REVISITING AND LEGALIZING 'ANTI-GAY' LAWS IN NIGERIA.
...a discussion on gay laws and the law prohibiting same-sex marriage in Nigeria.

REVISITING AND LEGALIZING 'ANTI-GAY' LAWS IN NIGERIA.

Written by:
GBENGA ODUGBEMI

© 2016 Bishops Publishing,
gbengaodugbemi@icloud.com
First published in 2016.

All rights reserved. No part of this publication may be reproduced, stored in a retrieval system, or transmitted in any form or by any means, electronic, mechanical, photocopying, recording or otherwise, without the prior permission of Bishops Publishing or its agent.

This publication is sold subject to the conditions that it shall not, by way of trade or otherwise be lent, resold, hired out, or otherwise circulated without the publisher's prior consent, in any form of binding or cover other than that in which it is published, and without a similar condition including this condition being imposed on any subsequent purchaser.

© 2016

Table of contents

Preface & Foreword	----------------	5-8
Acknowledgement	----------------	9
Dedication	----------------	10
The Controversy of Phobias	----------------	11
Working definition of LGBTQI	----------------	13-15

CHAPTER 1
FORE-NOTES/INTRODUCTION ------- 16-25

CHAPTER 2
THE RELEVANT LAWS ---------------- 26-60

CHAPTER 3
AN ASSESSMENT OF LAWS ON SAME-SEX RELATIONSHIP IN NIGERIA ---------------- 61-96

CHAPTER 4
OTHER ISSUES AND CONCLUSIONS ------ 97-105

CHAPTER 5
RECOMMENDATIONS, AND ARISING ISSUES -- 106-113

CHAPTER 6
THE RAMIFICATIONS OF LEGALIZING THE LGBT MOVEMENT IN NIGERIA -------------- 114-121

References	----------------	122-124
About the Author	----------------	125

Preface and Foreword

The Nigerian legislative contents must be agreed to be a developing one when compared to her counterparts even in Africa, and of course, countries in the west. The reason for the stagnancy of most of the laws is a by-product of the laziness of the Nigerian legislative arm. While some of the laws are beginning to be amended, the Nigerian legislature properly showed her position on the issue of LGBT in Nigeria via the Same Sex Marriage (Prohibition) Act in 2014. The latter law is not a product of a stagnant law, but a reiteration and advancement of some existing laws in the Criminal Code Act, and the Penal Code Act. This book examines all of these laws, in the Criminal Code Act, Penal Code Act, the provisions of Shari'a law and that of the SSMP. It thus presents a total dissection of all of the issues embedded in the LGBT discussions in Nigeria. The whole the SSMP Act, for example, is dissected to better explain points discussed. This book, therefore, represents a *locus classicus* on the LGBT discussion in Nigeria, making it essential for law students, lawyers, jurists, persons involved in the LGBT movement, and such other person seeking knowledge on the position of the law on LGBT in Nigeria.

I know, and it is possible to presume the idea contained in this book as supposing that the writer is an advocate of the LGBT movement in Nigeria, and wants the laws incriminating activities embedded in the movement decriminalized. This presumption is not entirely correct, in fact, what this book is about is a legal discussion of the laws incriminating the LGBT movement and the surrounding activities. It is a legal discussion, and as such only discussed the LGBT movement in relation to law, that is all. The main question is whether the laws incriminating the LGBT movement is legal or otherwise. By doing so, I placed the laws so incriminating the activities involved on a *legal pedestal* and construed it with well-accepted principles in law (in Nigeria), and such other laws existing in Nigeria. Upon doing this, we conclude whether the laws can be accepted or whether there is a need for annulment or amendment etc. In the course of doing this, other ambivalent provisions in the laws that need revisitation are highlighted.

Thus, this book must not be perceived as advocating for the LGBT movement or perceived as a support for the Nigerian government position on the issue. It is just a legal discussion, the side which thus tends to be correct between the LGBT movement and the Nigerian government can be discerned from a reading of the discussions contained therein.

The reluctance of Nigerian writers to address the topic since its main inception in 2014 is quite troubling, and the rationale(s) for this is somewhat discussed in the first chapter of the book, the highlighted justification is also challenged. I took it upon myself to write on the topic so that at least the populace interested or not interested in the topic could be aware of the position of the law on the issues. This book portrays not just the legal point of view of the LGBT movement, it contains a succinct overture into the Nigerian criminal laws – for the purpose of international readers. It also highlights some areas that need amendment in the highlighted criminal laws in Nigeria. It challenges the lackadaisical attitude of the Nigerian legislatures and hopes that changes would be made sometimes in the future.

Most persons involved in the LGBT movement in Nigeria lacks the arms needed to combat the government as regards their position in the society and the currently existing laws. To most of them, their counterparts in developed countries enjoy freedom via laws in those places, and they feel they should also be able to enjoy the same freedom as well, without looking into the provisions of the law in Nigeria.

This book is an *eye-opener* to persons involved in the LGBT movement, so they know the position of the law in Nigeria, especially what their basis of any challenge of any anti-gay law in Nigeria should be.

One issue I would like to mention here is the inclusion of the word "legalizing" in the title of the book. A legal colleague challenged the validity of the book title and concluded that it is inherently wrong in itself. He asserted that the subject in the title is "anti-gay laws", and asked how there would be a need to "legalize" a law. Also, that a law is already legal, and a call to legalize a law is incorrect and misleading. While I cannot dispute my colleague's argument as true, I nurture the belief that he has refused to see my argument from another perspective. In fact, our argument/discussion showed me that in an argument, two people could be right, and a bottle could be half full and half empty at the same time.

In my opinion, when I was deciding on the title of the book. My idea was to paint the "anti-gay laws" as illegal, and then, calling for their legalization – since what is illegal can only be made legal or totally abrogated, I chose the former. The next question then is: how can a law be illegal? It is very simple, for example, as it is currently, in criminal cases, the Nigerian Constitution (and in I believe every other jurisdiction in the world) necessitates a court hearing both parties – the prosecution and the accused – before handing a verdict, or at least that the accused be given an opportunity to defend himself. Now, consider a new law which states that "in a criminal action, only one party – the prosecutor – shall be allowed to address the court, and the defendant shall have no right of audience." If this provision is passed into law, like my colleague's argument, it becomes legal, but is that law truly legal? The answer is no.

The law is illegal because it offends prior existing law and well-established legal principles as *audi alterem partem* – that necessitates hearing both sides in an action/court hearing. If the earlier law supposing hearing both parties be heard had being abrogated before the new law, the legality of the new law would attract a new discussion entirely. My contention summarily is that a law which offends another existing law or which is unjust is illegal because "lex iniusta non est lex" – "an unjust law is no law at all". Hence, the need to find a way to legalize it – if it can, and that is the idea of the book title.

The "revisiting" idea in the title only called for some re-visitation of the relevant criminal provisions in the highlighted laws for reasons well-discussed in the book.

This writer welcomes another legal writer/commentator in Nigeria or elsewhere to write or communicate their disagreement as regards all or any of the assertions in this book. Questions as regards equivocal parts or areas in the book can also be communicated, I would try as much as possible to present clarifications. My contact could be found somewhere in this book. Permit me to also include that the use of web links was instrumental in this book of course, for obvious reason as the dearth of legal writings on the topic in Nigeria. Hopefully, this book would be a reference body for subsequent works on the topic.

Thank you.
Gbenga Odugbemi
30th September, 2016.

Acknowledgement

First, I acknowledge Monica Fatogun, she was the first to incite writing on this topic, and *Immigration Equality*, New York, for the *pro bono* opportunity that solidified my interest in writing on this topic. I also acknowledge the likes of Deji Owode (Esq.), Victor Ashonibare, Peter Ugbodaga, and Ernest Osaghae for their contrary, but interesting discussions on this topic, which they feel I must hear, no matter what. I also appreciate Eriyoma Ewharekuko for convincing me on writing the last chapter in this book; and the likes of Dapo Makinde, Taiwo Oyewande for their marketing strategies suggestions/stunts. I must also mention Jared Lewis Anesto for his art suggestions.

Thank you.

Dedication

This book is dedicated to **John Taylor Cameron**, *Lord Coulsfield* (24 April 1934 – 28 February 2016) – the man who gave me a legal education when I have no means to afford one.

The Controversy of Phobias

All phobias are characterized by 'fear', aside from one – often characterized with hate/dislike.

Acrophobia – The fear of heights.

Aerophobia – The fear of flying.

Monophobia – The fear of being alone

Phasmophobia – The fear of ghosts

Chronophobia – The fear of the future.

Photophobia – The fear of light

Homo(sexual)phobia – The fear of homosexuals?;

No, "the dislike of or prejudice against homosexual people"

'gbenga Odugbemi

Working -definition of LGBQTI

The definitions of personalities or states, which constitutes the LGBTQI is an evolving. The negative effect of that on work as this is that it would be hard to *pinpoint* a single definition of the personalities/states in LGBTQI. This explains why a *working definition* of the terms are first described at this early stage of the work. Whereas the definition herein might seem somewhat different (or not totally inclusive) from the conventional understanding of the terms, the description of the terms succinctly explained below are nonetheless close to conventional meaning. The meaning associated are as used in this work.

L – Lesbian
G – Gay
B – Bisexual
T – Transgender
Q – Queer
I – Intersex

Lesbian is a homosexual female. The attraction is between a woman and another woman.

Gay is used for homosexual persons generally; however, it is common to use 'gay' to refer to homosexual males. As commonly used, and as used in this work, the attraction is between a man and another man. So, we use 'gay' to refer to a homosexual male.

Bisexual, as the name implies is used for both male and female who have an attraction for persons of their own sex **and** the opposite sex. So, a female bisexual has an attraction for both a female like herself and a male – the opposite sex. A male bisexual has an attraction for a male as himself, and a female – the opposite sex.

Transgender, when someone is a transgender, such person has taken steps to change his physical features from what he or she was naturally assigned biologically, and from birth. The reasons for taking the steps for the gender re-assignment are enormous but important amongst them is that the *transgender* person believes innately that the gender he or she is being perceived as is not what he or she feels inside. So, a male person might feel innate that he is a female, and although the society might determine his gender by his genitalia (penis) at birth, he would exhibit feminine attributes, which could be perceived in his clothing, appearance, gesture, way of talking, and importantly, the desire to have sexual intercourse with another male (who he believes should have sex with her because he believes he is a female, and not what the society brands her because of his genitalia at birth). He would then take steps to reassign his gender from that of masculine to feminine. This might include several surgeries, ranging from removal of the determinant genitalia (penis), and creating an opening instead, using same as vagina, breast implantation (silicone gel implants are commonly used), removal of the Adam's apple etc, and such other removal/replacement needed to appear how he feels – feminine.

Queer is the umbrella term for those who are lesbians, gay/homosexual; insofar as such person is not straight/heterosexual or cisgender. Cisgender is the opposite of transgender, i.e. the person has the same gender identity as he/she has from birth.

Intersex, persons with the two sexual organs – penis and vagina – similar to hermaphroditism. It also covers those with an internal (reproductive) organ different from their external (sexual) organ. It's used in the former sense in this work.

CHAPTER 1

I understand, should a writer says he wouldn't commit a crime while writing for a minority in the society.

-gbenga Odugbemi

Fore-notes/Introduction

The laws on same sex marriage in Nigeria as notoriously decried, most especially by the West and other developed countries, international organizations, and of course Nigerian gays, lesbians, and bisexuals is not new as thought. There have been laws incriminating the act of "sexual intercourse"[1] to be precise amongst gays and lesbians especially, and the *surrounding acts* in Nigeria prior to the supposed "infamous" *"Same Sex Marriage (Prohibition) Act"* [hereinafter referred to as SSMP] that emerged in 2014.

Since this article wants to boast of an international flavour/colour, for readers not so conversant with criminal laws in Nigeria, here is a little background.

In practice, the way the criminal law operates in Nigeria is rather geographically-structured. What this means is that (for easier understanding), Nigeria should be seen as divided into the four cardinals – North, South, East, and West – for the purpose of the operation of criminal law. The Southern, Eastern, and Western part of Nigeria are governed by the

---

[1] Or having "carnal knowledge" as often termed, see section 214, Criminal Code Act.

"Criminal Code Act[2]". The Northern part (standing alone, and having more States than any of the other parts[3]) is governed by the "Penal Code (Northern States) Act"[4]. Now, because these legislation are Acts (and are made at the Federal level), it is only normal that the 36 States[5] falling within the cardinals further domesticate the (Federal) Act and make it a (State) Law, and applicable in the State[6]. So, a State in the North (having domesticated the Penal Code **Act**) will have a "Penal Code of State A[7]", while States in the other parts[8] (having domesticated the Criminal Code **Act**) will have "Criminal law of State B[9]". Thus, it is unusual to see a State in the East as Enugu citing Criminal Code *Act*, instead, a prosecutor in that State would cite "Criminal *Law* of Enugu State".

However, this sophistication must not be confused with the general applicability of laws in the 36 States in Nigeria; i.e. the description above should not be confused to mean that a State has to domesticate a Federal Act before same is

---

[2] 1916
[3] With 19 States
[4] 1960. In fact, the Criminal Code Act provisions are subject to that of the Penal Code Act (see section 1A of the Criminal Code Act), therefore allowing for the combined application of the two Acts in the relevant parts of the country.
[5] Nigeria has 36 States, and a Federal Capital Territory - Abuja
[6] This is the position in Nigeria as regards Criminal law and Penal Code
[7] "A" could be Kano State (a State in Northern Nigeria) or any other State in the Northern part of Nigeria
[8] i.e. West, South and East (excluding North)
[9] B could be Enugu State (a State in the Eastern part of Nigeria) or any other State in the East, South or Western part of Nigeria.

applicable in a Nigerian State. Such reasoning is incorrect, a Federal Act need not be always domesticated before it enjoys application in a Nigerian State. Often, the Federal Act in question defines which court has jurisdiction or not. Although Federal Act enjoys application usually in Federal (High) Courts[10], some Federal Acts defines courts having jurisdiction on interpreting it widely to include even State (High) Courts. For example, the EFCC Act[11] is a Federal Act, and "court" as defined under the Act includes Federal High Court (of course), but also includes State High Court, and High Court of the Federal Capital Territory, Abuja[12]. It means, that Federal Act by defining which "court" has jurisdiction confers same on all the courts mentioned earlier. Still, it should be noted, that "parties" still determine the "right" court to bring a case regardless[13], for example, it is unusual to see the Attorney-General of the Federation prosecuting a case under the EFCC Act in a State High Court. Usually, he would do so before the Federal (High) Court.

In our present discussion, the SSMP, (although a Federal Act) defines court as "High Courts" alone. In essence, only State High Courts in Northern, Southern, Eastern and

---

[10] Because of the parties involved, i.e. a Federal body – EFCC Commission
[11] Economic and Financial Crimes Commission Act, 2004
[12] See section 46 of the EFCC Act.
[13] And a Federal Court has jurisdiction on issues listed in section 251 of the Nigerian 1999 Constitution. These issues constitute constitutional "morass" and need not be explored in a work as this, so we do not deviate from the subject-matter of this book.

Western Nigeria have exclusive jurisdiction to try persons suspected of any of the proscribed acts under the Act[14].

Having explained this, as mentioned earlier, acts surrounding "sexual orientation" have already been dealt with (in the Criminal Code Act and Penal Code Act), although not as vast and as precise as do the SSMP. The legal provisions on "sexual orientation" and "gender identity" in Nigeria can thus (now) be seen from three laws – Criminal Code Act, Penal Code (Northern States Act), and the SSMP. However, as a writer grounded in some knowledge of Islamic law, it would be "incomplete" if Shari'a law's application as additionally adopted in some (Northern) States is not mentioned or included amongst laws making provisions for sexual orientation/gender identity in Nigeria. Shari'a law as it applies in the Northern States which have adopted it relies on the Penal Code Act of course, but with severe punishments[15]. So, it's *safer* to say, laws on sexual orientation and gender identity can be perceived from four laws in Nigeria, instead of from three laws.

Before examining the provisions of the laws, what they incriminate, and the punishment. It must be clarified from the outset what this work stands for.

---

[14] The High Court of the Federal Capital Territory, Abuja also has jurisdiction, but although Abuja is in Central Nigeria, the undertone of Northern laws applicability is "visible" there, so for *legal purpose*, Abuja could be said to be in Northern Nigeria.
[15] These harsh additions separates Shari'a law from ordinary Penal Code provisions in States which have adopted it in Northern Nigeria

First, this work refuse to take the side of the Nigerian government's initiative proscribing sexual orientation and same-sex marriage or that of the West or the LGBTQI community suggesting the *accommodation* and legality of freedom to choose one's identity or gender, including who to marry. Instead, the aim of this work is to examine the laws on the issue in Nigeria, and then conclude if they are legally viable or otherwise. This work relies on thoughts that: legislation in legal systems ought to be coherent; a new law should not oust an existing law (unless the existing law is repealed), that instead, the legislature should make laws with proper consideration of other existing laws. This work asks the question whether the four earlier cited laws proscribing freedom as to gender identity, sexual orientation, and same-sex marriage could co-exist with the various fundamental human rights already enshrined in several laws in Nigeria. If they can so co-exist, the research and examination reflects it; if they cannot so co-exist, this work thus suggests a "legal haven" (if any) for the laws incriminating sexual orientation, gender identity, and same-sex marriage in Nigeria, in a bid to *legalize* the concerned laws. In simple terms, considering the entire body of legislation in Nigeria, can a co-existence of laws (new or old) – incriminating sexual orientation, gender identity, and same-sex marriage still have a place?

If the answer is in the "affirmative", then the West, the Nigerian LGBTQI community, other developed countries, and international organizations should say no more, and must desist from further interfering with the laws incriminating sexual orientation and gender identity in

Nigeria. Importantly, they must also desist from "cajoling" the Nigerian government to dance to their tunes – allowing same-sex relationship; since such attitude can be interpreted to mean an assault on Nigeria's "sovereignty"[16] which includes the government's legal power to decide and make laws for her own people. However, if the answer is in the "negative", then the Nigerian government must "revisit" the laws incriminating sexual orientation, gender identity, same-sex marriage, and the surrounding acts. The reason is because, the co-existence of legislation suggesting freedom as regards sexual orientation, gender identity, and freedom from any discrimination, and other set of laws doing the reverse – incriminating same is a continuous air being blown into a balloon, ready to explode sometimes, whether the Nigerian government likes it or not. From another perspective, such co-existence place Nigeria some steps behind in her "legal development" before the world. How does a country explain the co-existence of laws approbating and reprobating at the same time?

This work respects the sovereignty of the Nigerian legislature to make laws for Nigeria, and of course, of the Nigerian government refusing to be *swayed* by the West and her cohorts to tamper with her beliefs as regards gender identity and sexual orientation – which ultimately expanded and incited the prohibition of same-sex marriages in Nigeria. This work is not, and should not be perceived as an *assault*

---

[16] One of the factors making a State "sovereign" is her ability to make laws for herself as it sees fit considering the local features without unnecessary interference from external forces.

on the laws on these issues, as it in no way challenges them. It also does not necessarily "support"[17] the acts proscribed in the relevant laws prohibiting same-sex relationship and surrounding acts. In lieu, as stated earlier, we are asking: "can these laws – incriminating same-sex relationships – exist considering other laws in Nigeria?". If not, the Nigerian legislature should take steps to revisit the law and "*legalize*"[18] it.

This writer is concerned about the scarcity of writings on this subject in Nigeria. In this writer's view, the lackadaisical attitude of Nigerian writers on this subject, and the dearth of works on it is an upshot of three things. One, the SSMP radically unlike the previous the provisions in the previous three laws, further incriminates "support" of same-sex relationship in a technical manner[19]. Thus, since one cannot advocate for the LGBTQI movement without referring to their legal freedom to associate as expounded in the Nigerian Constitution, writers are wary that their writings might be interpreted as "supporting" what the Act directly incriminates. Truly, for simple and obvious reasons, as it is

---

[17] It must be noted that a suggestive "support" of what the Same Sex Marriage (prohibition) Act prohibits is also a crime under the Act, see section 5(3). Since this writer is still a Nigerian, I do not intend to incriminate myself.

[18] "Legalize" as used here is predicated on the fact that, if the new law (incriminating same-sex marriage), and other laws incriminating sexual orientation and gender identity cannot be sustained construing other existing laws in Nigeria, then the former laws are "illegal". Hence, the Nigerian legislature should "legalize" them – which would definitely mean/necessitate an amendment.

[19] See section 5(3) of the Act

currently, without debating on whether the "SSPM" is a "bad law" or a "good law"[20], a "support" of what the Act incriminates would be *sufficient* as a basis of prosecution in Nigeria, since there's a law incriminating such "support". This is in tune with the provisions of section 36(12) of the Nigerian 1999 Constitution[21].

It could be reasoned that, in the negative, a writing or comment might not "support" what the SSMP incriminates. In essence, that writers could write not necessarily what would advance a "support" of what the SSPM proscribe, that they can write in a bid to confirm their "disagreement" of allowing same-sex relationships as do the SSPM. This leads us to another reason why Nigerian writers avoid this subject. No legal writer/commentator (with basic and/or adequate knowledge of the law) could possibly write in *disagreement* of allowance or legality of same-sex relationship in Nigeria, as doing so would amount to "academic

---

[20] Arguments filled with the continuous friction between "Positive" and "Natural law" theories in Legal Jurisprudence – a "battle" which Positive law School seems to have been winning consistently.

[21] The Constitution provides that: "Subject as otherwise provided by this Constitution, a person shall not be convicted of a criminal offence unless that offence is defined and the penalty therefore is prescribed in a written law, and in this subsection, a written law refers to an Act of the National Assembly or a Law of a State, any subsidiary legislation or instrument under the provisions of a law." Thus, since there is an Act – a "written law" – (of the National Assembly) – "Same Sex Marriage (Prohibition) Act, 2014" – incriminating "support" of what that Act incriminates, and since same is defined in section 5(3) of the Act, the punishment inclusive, as 10 years imprisonment; then a writer who writes in "support" risk being convicted in line with constitutional provisions.

dishonesty". From a superficial look, there is almost no absolute "hanger" a legal writer or commentator could hang the radical SSPM Act or similar provisions in the law, even in Nigeria. If such absolute "hanger" exists, this writer challenges (in a polite way) such writer's/commentator's "reply" to this work with a discussion on such absolute "hanger".

In any way, writers are pre- technically coerced to write in "support" of what the SSPM incriminates, and any writing or comment that does otherwise would amount to "academic dishonesty". To thus avoid this, legal writers/commentators just avoid the issue in totality[22]. Brusquely, for a Nigerian writer, the case is a dilemma. He finds himself in a serious impasse. If he writes in a way that challenges the SSMP, this can be viewed as a crime under section 5(3) of the SSMP. I understand, should a writer says he wouldn't commit a crime while writing for a minority in the society[23]. On the other hand, if he writes to agree with

---

[22] This seem as a "betrayal" of how writers should position themselves in a *developing* country as Nigeria. As *Achebe* described in his Autobiography: "My own assessment is that the role of a writer is not a rigid position and depends to some extent on the state of health of his or her society. In other words, if a society is ill, the writer has the responsibility to point it out. If the society is healthier, the writer's job is different" See: *"There Was A Country (A Personal History of Biafra)"*, Chinua Achebe, Penguin Books, 2012; at page 57.

[23] The situation is similar to that of Christopher Okigbo, a fervent writer during the agitation of Biafra break-away from Nigeria in the 1960's. Christopher left writing to join the (Biafran) Army, and was killed. Later, *Ali Mazrui*, commenting on Christopher's life in his *"The Trial of Christopher Okigbo"* sees Christopher to have wasted "his

the SSMP, there is almost no absolute "hanger" to "hang" that law considering other laws pre-existing and still existing in Nigeria, and before the world. Thus, a writer who chooses to agree with the SSMP risks losing credibility as a writer/commentator.

Lastly, the majority of legal writers/commentators in Nigeria recluse from this subject and allow foreigners to comment on it because they personally carry the idiosyncrasies bestowed on them by religion and morality common and embedded in Nigerian cultures. Legal writers/commentators have refused to address sexual orientation, gender identity issues, same-sex marriage and the law, because the society they grow up in, their background, and almost all Nigerian cultures frown at it anyway. While this is understandable, still, the line must be drawn between law and personal beliefs, religion, culture or even morality.

---

great talent on a conflict of disputable merit" – The Nigerian Civil War and all its ramified implications, that is. He further charged Christopher to have put the society before art in his scale of values, and concluded that: no artist has a right to carry patriotism to the extent of destroying his creative potentials". See: Ali Mazrui, "*The Trial of Christopher Okigbo*", African Writers Series (London: Heinemann 1971).

CHAPTER 2

The 'order of nature' is carnal knowledge with the female sex. Carnal knowledge with the male sex is against the order of nature and here, nature should mean God…it is possible I am wrong in my superlative extension of the expression.

-Per Tobi, JSC, in Magaji vs. The Nigerian Army

The Relevant Laws

As mentioned earlier, the *res* of criminal laws on sexual orientation, gender identity, and surrounding acts can be found in four corpus of laws – the Criminal Code Act, The Penal Code Act, Shar'ia law, and the recent SSMP Act. Of course, while the provisions are somewhat dissimilar in terms of descriptions of acts they incriminate, and the severity of punishments for such acts, still, there is a resonating similar attribute amongst these laws. The similar attribute is that all of these laws refuse to allow same-sex relationship, and every surrounding act(s).

The Criminal Code Act:
This law was promulgated and became law on the 1st of June, 1916; that is like 100 years calculated from when the law is promulgated and the publication of this work. Definitely, Nigeria must be one of the countries with the oldest (unamended) criminal law in practice. Whether this is a good thing or a bad thing depends on how one views it. For example, that the law is 100 years old (unamended) does not mean newer crimes which are not dealt with in the law are not being dealt with today. In Nigeria, there are several

other laws – with some provisions incriminating certain acts, the EFCC Act contains such incriminating provisions, even the Companies, and Allied Matters Act[24] make some acts a crime, and the list goes on. However, just above the latter argument is the *backlash*. There is a need for a criminal law codification as the Criminal Code Act, and a *continuous* amendment of the law – so that the law can reflect societal changes, develop, and accommodate newer crimes. Hundred years is just too long not have amended a criminal law of a country.

As a Nigerian lawyer, I am not aware of any time this law has been amended or repealed or anything done to it, the law has been like that, incriminating acts contained therein, for a century. In an attempt not to digress, as earlier mentioned, there had been provisions restricting same-sex relationships, choosing one's gender or sexuality before the SSMP. This law (Criminal Code Act) must be the first to incriminate the surrounding acts since it has been in force since 1916, earlier before the Penal Code (Northern States) Act, which only came into force in 1966. In its Chapter 21 titled: "Offence against morality", section 214 first opened the idea of what is considered "immoral" and considered a crime.

For easy referencing, it provides:
    "*Any person who-*
    (1) has **carnal knowledge** *of any person* **against the order of nature;** *or*

---

[24] 1990

> *(2) has carnal knowledge of an animal; or*
>
> *(3)* **permits a male person** *to have carnal knowledge of* **him or her against the order of nature;**
>
> *is guilty of a felony, and is liable to imprisonment for fourteen years."*

[Emphasis added]

Definitely, it appears that only subsections 1 and 3 are relevant to our discussions as subsection 2 deals with bestiality. There has been no "loud" agitation about the wrongfulness and criminal nature of bestiality (for now at least). Thus, considering the relevant subsections and especially the words in bold prints. It must be pointed out that while the Criminal Code Act defines what "carnal knowledge" means, it has refused to define what the most important phrase – "against the order of nature" – means or should mean in the context of the law. Perhaps, if the law had defined this *controlling* phrase, the position might be different today. The laxity of the law however in not defining this phrase necessitates the Judiciary to be active, and not passive in their interpretation of the provision. No doubt, the said judicial activism would previously (when the law was written) almost be straight-forward; but today, that judicial task would be hard, considering the fact that what is "order of nature" has now today proven to be elusive.

The attitude of the legislature in refusing to define this phrase is understandable, it could be reasoned to be that then (when the law was written) that phrase is only capable of a *sole* interpretation. Especially since, even in the West, homosexuality was recently legally decriminalized.

Fortunately, the Supreme Court of Nigeria has had an opportunity to pronounce on similar sections before in 2008.

In *Major Bello Magaji vs. The Nigerian Army*[25], a case involving sodomy in the Army. The accused was charged under the Armed Forces Decree[26], section 81. Section 81 (although subsequent subsections under it are collectively defined as "Sodomy") is, in fact, a carbon copy of section 214(1) of the Criminal Code Act, so the interpretation of the court is applicable here as well. The court reasoned that:

"The Armed Forces Decree does not define carnal knowledge. Section 6 of the Criminal Code Act defines carnal knowledge or the term carnal connection. The term implies that the offence, so far as regards that element of it, is complete upon penetration. While carnal knowledge is an old legal euphemism for sexual intercourse with a woman, it acquires a different meaning in section 81. The section 81 meaning comes to light when taken along with the proximate words 'against the order of nature'. **The order of nature is carnal knowledge with the female sex. Carnal knowledge with the male sex is against the order of nature** and here, nature should mean God and not just the generic universe that exists independently of mankind or

---

[25] S.C. 204/2004
[26] 1993

people. **It is possible I am wrong in my superlative extension of the expression.** As that will not spoil the merits of the judgment, I leave it at that."
[Emphasis added]

The above *dicta* which contributed to the *ratio* of the decision held in that case is quite well-informed. With the knowledge of what "carnal knowledge" means and "the order of nature", the provisions of section 214 is more than clear.

However, it must be pointed out that the most relevant subsection in section 214 is its subsection 1, subsection 3 only applies partly. The reason is because considering the issues constituting *agitation* – LGBTQI – subsection 3 defines something closer to "Sodomy", and not entirely what we are discussing in this work or what is causing *agitation*. In fact, subsection 1 provides a total idea of what we are discussing. A proper reading of subsection 3 shows two things. One, "Any person", let's assume the person here is a female, who permits a male person to have carnal knowledge of her against the 'order of nature' – has committed an offence. This is the first interpretation of subsection 3 since that subsection used the fixed term "male". In essence, this first interpretation implies sodomy, because the sexual intercourse is between a female and a male – this itself would mean complying with the "order of nature", but in the course of doing that, if the parties engage in anal or oral copulation[27], then that would be against the

---

[27] See the Black's Law Dictionary, 2nd Edition, that uses "Anal Copulation"

"order of nature". It implies that the "order of nature" is wide when reading subsection 3.

The other interpretation, and why we say subsection 3 is partly relevant to our discussion is this. "Any person", let's assume the person here is a male, who permits a male person to have carnal knowledge of him against the 'order of nature' – has committed an offence. Here, both the carnal knowledge between two males is being incriminated since that ordinarily is considered "against the order of nature"– this would fall on the 'G' in L**'G'**BTQI. Even if the parties do not engage in oral or anal copulation, their intercourse (carnal knowledge) alone is sufficient to constitute a crime. This is why only a part of subsection 3 is relevant.

However, considering subsection 1, which provides that: "anyone who has carnal knowledge of any person against the order of nature…" This section alone incriminates being gay and being a lesbian – that is "**LG**"BTQI. For B, Q and I, subsection 1 incriminates their conducts as well. Since being a Bisexual implies ability to have carnal knowledge of both sexes – male or female; it means, if a male is bisexual, he would only have committed a crime if his conduct is such that he had carnal knowledge of another male – which would be considered as against the 'order of nature'; if he had carnal knowledge of a female – which is he is also capable of – he has not committed a crime[28]. For Q also

---

[28] Note that although we deduce our understanding of "order of nature" from the *Magaji*'s case, this section and its interpretation must be understood in the light of subsection 1, and not subsection

which is an umbrella term, it would appear that if a Queer has a male genitalia, and has carnal knowledge of a female, his conduct wouldn't have constituted a crime here, but if as he is, he had carnal knowledge of another man, he would be guilty. For intersex, the situation is complex, the prosecutor must prove the accused/suspect is using either of his genitalia to have carnal knowledge of the other against the 'order of nature'. The T's case – Transgender – is not provided for, and can't be *squeezed* in, discussions in this regard would unfold later.

The last thing that must be noted as regards section 214 is that in the most relevant subsection, which is subsection 1, the other person at the end of the intercourse would not be liable for homosexuality. So if it is A who had carnal knowledge of B, from the literal interpretation of that subsection and as do the Supreme Court in the case cited earlier, A is the only one who would be liable; B would not be liable. It is confusing whether this is the intention of the legislature as regards this provisions, but this interpretation appears as the 'literal' interpretation. If another intention is intended (which is probable), then, the Nigerian legislature must *revisit* that section entirely, and make corrections.

The reasoning of the interpretation/proposition for amendment here finds refuge in similar interpretation in rape cases as well, where the person being raped is passive, and not a criminal. Section 357 of the Criminal Code Act provides that: "Any person who has unlawful carnal

---

3 as defined in the case.

knowledge of a woman or girl, without her consent, or with her consent…", it is the former person [the subject] who commits rape, since he is the one who has carnal knowledge of another, forcefully or unlawfully. In our discussion too, where we have: "any person who has carnal knowledge of another against the order of public…", the only person who seems to be liable would be the former person as well. How this interpretation makes sense in respect of two homosexuals (engaging in sexual intercourse) and the law punishing just one of them – the domineering party as one would expect – is not only questionable, it's confusing, and *opens the door* for acts that are intended to be 'crimes'.

Having said that, still in light of the *legal creation*[29] of domineering and receiving party during sexual intercourse. In subsection 3 discussed above, it seems "a male who **permits** another male…" would be liable, even though he is at the other end of the intercourse, this is because subsection 3 uses the word "permits". The *permission* envisaged by the provision *opened the door* for the recipient of the intercourse to liability as well. So, for being gay[30], both parties would be 'liable' (under subsection 3, not 1); but for being a lesbian,

---

[29] It would be a 'legal creation' for the purpose of understanding these sections, because, ordinarily, during sexual intercourse, there is no domineering or receiving party, what we have is two people having sex

[30] Note the explanation and the meaning attributed to being 'gay' at the early page of this book. 'Gay' is used herein to refer to 'homosexual male'.

only one party would likely be liable, under subsection 1, since a lesbian can't be liable under subsection 3[31].

Another relevant section under the Criminal code Act is section 215 that makes an *attempt* to commit acts described in section 214 punishable as well. Such inchoate act amounting to an "attempt" is punishable with 7 years imprisonment.

The last relevant section which is on *'surrounding acts'* is section 217, it provides that: *"Any **male** person who, whether in public or private, **commits** any act of **gross indecency with another male person**, or **procures** another male person to commit any act of gross indecency with him, or **attempts** to procure the commission of any such act by any male person with himself or with another male person, whether in public or private, is guilty of a felony, and is liable to imprisonment for three years..."*
[Emphasis added]

Under the LGBTQI, it is clear that this latter provision is restricted to male only. It thus deals with the G, unless a B or Q who is a male engage in the act as well, but it does not extend to 'L' – lesbians. The question is: can we say lesbians can engage in what a Nigerian court would consider "gross indecency"?. Clearly, with the emergence of time, and a law as the SSMP, this cannot truly represent the view of the Nigerian legislature today. This section calls for a re-

---

[31] We said this under the notion that a 'lesbian' ordinarily would not ordinarily allow a 'male' have carnal knowledge of her – since that is what makes her a 'lesbian', and not 'bisexual'

visitation so that the intention of the legislature would be clearly known. At best, a particular feature of a criminal law is that it should be really clear, unequivocal, and free from ambiguity. The current instance where lesbians in Nigeria are being maltreated in public under the law should be stopped since this law do not seem to contemplate such. The SSMP cannot be used to justify the maltreatment as well since that law borders on making a union of persons of similar sex illicit.

However, it must be noted that "gross indecency" is a low standard – used as a legislative decoy to capture every surrounding acts around homosexuality. The issues involved in LGBTQI are way higher and would most likely fall within what a Nigerian court would consider "gross indecency", especially if the surrounding acts embedded in the LGBTQI community are expressed in public. The problem with this section that would fall for consideration in the next part of this work is its incrimination of what male persons (which it literally attacks) do in **private** – if we agree that acts which constitute **public** gross indecency are unlawful. Also, if we agree especially that the legislature has a duty to prevent **public** morals by virtue of the constitution[32]. We must consider acts done in the **private,** against the background of the *right to privacy* of Nigerian citizens, despite their sexual orientation.

---

[32] See: section 45(1)(a), Nigerian 1999 Constitution

Penal Code (Norther States) Act:

The Penal Code (Northern States) Act is the second legislation (sequel to the Criminal Code Act) making provisions for the incrimination of sexual orientation and surrounding acts. There are three relevant sections closely identical to that of the Criminal Code Act. The first relevant section is under Chapter XVIII titled "Offences Affecting the Human Body", section 284. It reads:

*"Whoever has **carnal intercourse against the order of nature** with a man, woman or an animal, shall be punished with imprisonment for a term of which may extend to fourteen years **and shall also be liable to fine."***
[Emphasis added]

This provision is closely similar to section 214 of the Criminal Code Act discussed above, so it adopts the discussions therein. Also, considering the abbreviation LGBTQI, we adopt the explanation especially that: this provision also incriminates acts surrounding being a lesbian, gay, and bisexual or queer which are considered against the 'order of nature'. The only difference is that, whereas the punishment under these two laws is similar – 14 years imprisonment – the present law also necessitates payment of fine **in addition** to the prison term. The two punishments – possible prison term, and payment of fine both run together when a person is found guilty since the law uses the conjunctive word "and" and a rather obligatory word – "Shall"[33].

---

[33] See: SEPLAT PETROLEUM DEVELOPMENT v. BRITTANIAU NIGERIA

Just by way of digressing, but adding to knowledge. There is a common misconception amongst people not well-acquainted with the law, and misunderstanding amongst those so acquainted about a sentencing that a person should pay fines in respect of a criminal charge. The misconception/misunderstanding is that when a court asks a party to pay just fines, he is not a criminal. This reasoning is wrong, if a person is charged with a crime, and the court orders the person to pay a fine, the person is just a criminal as a person sentenced to a certain jail term. In fact, in criminal law, a charged person becomes a criminal, not when the sentence is passed, but when the court finds the person guilty, and maybe ask for allocution, often in court's discretion.

Back to the foregoing discussion, a similar section to section 217 of the Criminal Code Act describe above is section 285 of the Penal Code (Northern States) Act which incriminates conducts described as "gross indecency". It must be noted that the *spirit* of this two provisions is similar but with different wordings, and especially that the Penal Code (Norther States) Act's provisions are vast. It provides:

"Whoever commits an act of **gross indecency** *upon the person of another* **without his consent** *or by the use of force* **or** *threats* **compels a person to join with him in the commission of that act,** *shall be punished with imprisonment for a term which may*

LIMITED & ORS, Suit No: CA/L/100/2014; the Court of Appeal reasoned that: "the word 'shall' when used in a statutory provision imports that a thing **must** be done..."

*extend to seven years **and shall also be liable to fine:** Provided that a consent given by a person below the age of sixteen years to such an act when done by his teacher, guardian or a person entrusted with his care or education shall not be deemed to be a consent within the meaning of this section".*

While this provision is similar to section 217 of the Criminal Code, the similarity starts and ends with the fact that "gross indecency" is incriminated; and as stated earlier, it is unlikely that acts surroundings LGBTQI would be considered below the standard of "gross indecency" in Nigeria. Aside from this, it might be possible to argue that the ways the two sections are drafted, it is only one person who would be liable for the commission of the offence described. Since the provisions are subjective, and not encompassing all of those involved. This is true of course when a person commits or compels another (by the use of force or threat) to engage in acts constituting "gross indecency" with **him** (not her) under the Penal Code Act. Clearly, both provisions commence with wordings as: "Whoever" and "Any male" (as used in the Penal Code and Criminal Code Act respectively). The other party at the receiving end would likely not be liable as the description of the offence focus entirely on the subject of the person engaging in the act with a total absence of reference to the other party. As mentioned earlier, it is doubtful whether this position can still be maintained with what the Nigerian legislature is trying to say today via the SSMP.

If the Nigerian government via her legislature wants to incriminate acts surrounding LGBTQI, a law or provision as this making one of the parties susceptible to prosecution is not only unfair, it fails to appreciate the current situation of the issues

Aside from the on-going discussions still, there are four other issues about the two provisions that must be noted.

One, the Criminal Code Act makes "gross indecency" a crime capable of being committed by a male alone[34], whereas, the Penal Code (Northern States) Act uses "Whoever" – which is more encapsulating, i.e. comprising of both male and female. It is unclear why the Criminal Code Act restrict acts constituting "gross indecency" to be such capable of being committed by a male alone perhaps for some reasons. However, for whatever reason it is, it's agreeable to say that the provision does not reflect today's developments. The Penal Code (Norther Provisions) Act could be said to represent more of what the Nigerian government is trying to say today via the SSMP. However, it seems also that only a "male" person could commit the acts considered "gross indecency" under the Penal Code Act as well. The Criminal Code Act is more explicit when it commences with "any male". The Penal Code is explicit too, when one reads it very well, and not confused with the use of "whoever" at its commencement. The idea of "whoever" encompassing both male and female possible liability was taking away within the description of the crime itself –

---

[34] See: section 217, Criminal Code Act

"*compels a person to join with **him** in the commission of that act…*". Reading the criminal provision thus becomes very controversial, because the crime description starts with "whoever", but contains the undertone of masculinity alone.

Secondly, as mentioned earlier, the Criminal Code Act incriminates what constitutes "gross indecency" committed in privacy – an issue that would be discussed later – but the Penal Code Act is silent on where the "gross indecency" is being committed. It is, therefore, reasonable to say that the *silence* of the Penal Code Act would be interpreted as incriminating acts constituting "gross indecency" irrespective of where same is committed – public or private. This reasoning is not far-fetched, considering another offence with such *silence* on the *place of commission* – the offence of "Theft" – as defined in section 286 of the Penal Code Act. The provision reads: "Whoever, intending to take dishonestly any movable property out of the possession of a person without that person's consent, moves that property, in order to take it, is said to commit theft."

From the above provision, where the "taking" occurs is not made mention of, whether private or public. It would, therefore, make no difference whether the "taking" occurred in private or public. This is the type of provision made under section 285 of the Act as well, and similar interpretation hence follows. Thus, both provisions of the Criminal Code Act and the Penal Code Act are thus similar, since the former Act incriminates acts constituting the offence committed in "public or private" anyway. The two provisions must thus be subject to an assessment on whether considering the *res* of laws in Nigeria, a criminal law can regulate sexual conducts, done in private.

It is also noteworthy that under the Penal Code Act, a light of *development* illuminated as regards persons who engage in what would constitute "gross indecency". In fact, a proper reading of section 285 would show that the person engaged in the act who would have been liable, would not be if the person at the *receiving end*/victim had given consent[35]. This, in fact, is one of the arguments of the West and other international communities, gays, lesbians and everyone supporting the LGBTQI movement – that what is incriminated should not be if the parties involved are **"consenting"** adults[36]. The Penal Code Act even represents this the more when it obviates the possibility of a child below the age of 16 from being able to give such consent – because he/she is not considered an 'adult'. Whereas this position is not often cited when describing Nigeria before the world as a country that forbids surrounding acts around LGBTQI, the provision alone is quite refreshing and positive. Still, the refreshing nature of this provision must be read with other provisions of the law in whole, and the overall reflection is in the negative.

---

[35] And the subject do not introduce another person into the act, or even if he does, if he did not use force or threat to compel such other person to join him in the act, and the victim (above 16 years old in the situation described) gives consent all through

[36] See Josh Sager's discussions in "Refuting Anti-Gay Rights Argument" available at: https://theprogressivecynic.com/debunking-right-wing-talking-points/refuting-anti-gay-rights-arguments/

Lastly, the Penal Code Act mandates a fine in addition to the 7 years imprisonment when an act is found to constitute "gross indecency". This is a wider punishment than that prescribed in the Criminal Code Act.

The last relevant provisions in the Penal Code Act as regards LGBTQI are section 405, and section 407 – that prescribes punishment for the act described in section 405. Rather radically, being a "vagabond" is a crime in the North and under the Penal Code Act, one of the acts described under section 405 as constituting being a "vagabond" touches on the issues we are discussing.

In section 405(2)(e), the Act provides that: "The term "vagabond" shall include: **any male person** who dresses or is attired in the fashion of a woman in a public place…" In the LGBTQI realm, the term "vagabond" as described by the Penal Code Act, section 405(2)(e) would fit more as "transvestite" or person in the transgender process – a male dressing like a female to reflect what he feels or considers himself to be. Although the literal English meaning of a "transvestite" might suggest that a male dressing in female apparels do so because he derives "pleasure" by doing so. In the LGB**'T'**QI situation, he dresses as do a female because he feels he is a female, pleasure is thus a mere part of what he feels, the driving factor actually is instead his keen desire to appear and become female. This feeling and desire often lead to such male undergoing a series of transgender surgeries or other required processes – all in order for him to become female. Thus, if a transgender man could undergo surgeries to look like a female, mere wearing feminine dress would definitely not be a *big* issue.

The case of one Dapo Adaralegbe[37] is instructive in explaining this issue. One *summary* described him as when he was in school (before getting expelled), that although he is a male, "he never dressed as a male"[38]. The point being made by the Penal Code Act is that the mere dressing of a male in female apparel is a crime of being a "vagabond", punishable under section 407 with imprisonment which may extend to 2 years or a fine up to N450[39] or even both. It is thus clear that the Dapo's case could have gone or be successful in a court in the South-Western part of Nigeria where he (now she) used to dress as a female, most likely because the Criminal Code Act applicable in the South/Western Nigeria do not incriminate transvestites[40] as do the Penal Code. His behavior, and that of others in relation to male dressing as a female in other parts of Nigeria, aside the North, must, therefore, be accepted as licit, unless the Criminal Code Act is revisited, but until then.

---

[37] a Nigerian student who has now being forced to live in Spain, of course by several factors including, critics, abandonment, fear of his life being taken etc
[38] See: http://thestreetjournal.org/2012/02/nigerian-professors-homosexual-son-becomes-woman-in-spain/
[39] See section 407 of the Penal Code (Northern States) Act. It provides: Whoever is convicted as being a vagabond shall be punished with imprisonment which may extend to two years or with fine which may extend to four hundred and fifty naira or both.
[40] An attribute of a transgender person

One important issue about this provision, however, is that the Penal Code Act fix the crime of transvestism as being capable of commission by a male alone. The reason for this is also unclear, it's thus clearly arguable that in the North, a female dressing as a male cannot be subjected to prosecution. The question again is: can the undertone of this interpretation find refuge within the idea of renunciation of LGBTQI as Nigeria currently portray?

It must be said that this provision and others restricting persons capable of committing crimes to male alone represents an argument suggesting sexism within the law in Nigeria as do the provisions on rape as well. The male gender is often subjected to prosecution by criminal law than the female. We have cited several of these instances in this work, especially the provision for rape – whereby only a male is considered capable of having sexual intercourse with a female without her consent. The position should be vice-versa as in developed countries which constantly revisit and amend their criminal laws.

If transvestism would be incriminated in the North, it should be done in a way that gives consideration to both sexes; but no one wants to see a female being dragged to jail for wearing a trouser or wearing a masculine shirt. This, in fact, represents the first hypocrisy in the abdication of the LGBTQI in Nigeria, and partly in the feminist theory. So, a male dressing like a female can be a criminal, but vice versa, the attitude would be licit. In a true sense of equality as feminist suggests, and as equity in law suggest, the same reason why females are allowed to wear men's clothing should be the same reason why males should be allowed to the same.

The Shari'a Law

The position of Shari'a law in Nigeria is a very controversial one being that it is religious based[41]. A look at section 10 of the Nigerian 1999 Constitution often points to the fact that Nigeria is a secular state. Section 10 reads: "The Government of the Federation or of a State shall not adopt any religion as State Religion." However, a proper reading of this provision do not necessarily mean the Nigerian government is forbidden from giving preference to a religion as Islam or Christianity – the two predominant religions in the country or even that Nigeria is a secular State. What the provision merely intend in simple terms is that: the Government should refrain from adopting a religion as a "State religion". One can reason that this provision further creates the platform for section 38 on "Right to freedom of religion" amongst other things.

Still, the constitution itself and the practice of the Nigerian government seems to place some deference on Islam than Christianity. In practice, Nigeria is a member of major

---

[41] Shari'a or Islamic law "is based on the Islamic religion, and was introduced in Nigeria as a consequence of a successful process of Islamization. It is based on the Holy Koran and the teachings of the Prophet Mohammad." See: Jadesola Lokulo-Sodipe, Oluwatoyin Akintola, Clement Adebamowo, "Introduction to the legal system of Nigeria", 2014. Available at: http://elearning.trree.org/mod/page/view.php?id=142

Moslem international organizations in the world[42], in fact, the President just hosted a conference in the Federal Capital Territory, having an "Islamic character" — although it is aimed at peace and stability in the country[43]. The Constitution also seems to give some deference to Shari'a/Islamic law when it creates Shari'a courts and name them superior courts of record[44].

From other Islamic law scholars, I have listened to arguments as that a Shari'a court is justified under the Nigerian Constitution because a large percentage of the country's population are Moslems. Also that the Koran, and the teachings of Muhammad (SAW) prescribes a way of life, and describes punishments on facets of lives of Moslems. In essence, Shari'a law can be seen as a personal law (describing the way of life for Moslems, and the consequence if one strays). The argument continues that in contrast, the Ko'ran's counterpart — the Bible, and even Jesus Christ — have failed to do the same in a *concise* manner as do the Ko'ran, and the Islamic prophet — Muhammad (SAW). The validity of arguments as these is not the crux of this work, in any way, this author is merely finding the basis (in law) where we could place Shari'a or Islamic law in Nigeria. This

---

[42] E.g., Organization of Islamic Cooperation, Islamic Development Bank, Organization of Islamic Conference

[43] President Muhammadu Buhari recently hosted an International Islamic conference in Abuja; see: http://www.vanguardngr.com/2016/03/photos-buhari-hosts-international-islamic-conference-in-abuja/

[44] See sections 6(5)(f) and (g) creating two courts having jurisdiction in Shari'a law; and section 6(3) making these courts alongside others "courts of superior records"

is necessary especially since there have been arguments that Islamic law/Shari'a law is not the same as Customary law[45], and it is rather notorious in the Nigerian legal system that Customary laws are applicable in Nigeria if such law passes the "repugnant tests"[46].

Understanding that the Supreme Court of Nigeria in *Alkamawa v Bello*[47] pronounced that Islamic law as not the same as customary law, and that it is a complete system of universal law, and more universal than the English Common Law; we must agree that Islamic law stands alone in Nigeria, but only in the North. We say in the North because a more likely "basis" of Shari'a law one can place a hand on in Nigeria is in section 2 of the High Court Law, Cap. 49, **Laws of Northern Nigeria**[48].

---

[45] See: Y. K Saadu, *"Islamic Law is NOT Customary Law"*, 1997 Kwara Law Review, Vol. 6. See also: L. A. Kelani, "Islamic Law and the Customary/Native Law: A Line of Distinction", Unilorin Shariah Journal, Vol. 1, Dec 2000

[46] A customary law practice is subject to tests before it is applicable in a Nigerian court. The tests are that: "the customary law is not repugnant to natural justice, equity and good conscience, and that such customary law must not be incompatible either directly or by implication with any law for the time being in force." See also: section 16 of the Evidence Act Cap 214 Laws of the Federation of Nigeria 2011 that supports this tests (partly). It provides that: "Provided that in case of any custom relied upon in any judicial proceeding, it shall not be enforced as law if it is contrary to public policy and is not in accordance with natural justice, equity and good conscience." See also *Okonkwo v Okagbue* (1994) 9 NWLR (368).

[47] (1998) 6 S.C.N.J. 127. See also: A.I. ABIKAN, *"THE APPLICATION OF ISLAMIC LAW IN CIVIL CAUSES IN NIGERIAN COURTS"*, Journal of International and Comparative Law, (June 2002) 6 JICL. Pages 88-115.

[48] 1963

Moving beyond the validity and application of Shari'a law in the Northern part of Nigeria (where it is only applicable), we must then consider what it says about LGBTQI and the acts surrounding it. It must first be understood that only 12 states [out of the 19 to which the Penal Code (Northern States) Act applies] adopt the application of Shari'a law in Northern Nigeria. The 12 States are often further divided into two. A category believes or supposes that **all** her State residents are Moslems[49], and the other believes or carries a supposition that only a **majority** of her residents are Moslems[50]. For the latter category, it is the "notion" that majority of her residents are Moslems that in fact operates as the rationale behind the adoption and application of Shari'a law by those States.

The provisions of Shari'a law on issues surrounding LGBTQI is straight-forward, although often clothed with "sodomy". A typical example of the provisions is section 130 and 131 of the Zamfara State of Nigeria Shari'a Penal Code Law (2000)[51]. Section 130 provides that:

"130. Whoever has carnal intercourse **against the order of nature** *with any man* **or woman** *is said to commit the offence of sodomy:*

---

[49] These Moslem plurality states includes: Gombe, Kaduna and Niger State
[50] These include: Zamfara, Kano, Sokoto, Katsina, Bauchi, Borno, Jigawa, Kebbi, and Yobe State.
[51] Same is available at: www.f-law.net/law/showthread.php/37487-Shari-ah-Penal-Code-Law-Zamfara-State-Of-Nigeria-January-2000

Provided that whoever is **compelled by the use of force or threats or without his consent** *to commit the act of sodomy upon the person of another or be the subject of the act of sodomy,* **shall not be deemed** *to have committed the offence."*
[Emphasis added]

This definition section adopts the same explanation given to "order of nature", and what constitute "against the order of nature" as earlier discussed above. It, therefore, adopts the expositions and critiques given above. Thus, a proper reading of or an argument that could emanate from section 130 also is that it's just one party who would be a suspect. If the receiving party consents, it is unclear if such person would be liable as well (within the purview of this provisions). Argument as "Golden-rule" interpretation of the provision that could be applied so that the purpose of this section is not defeated is not totally true, especially since the *literal rule* interpretation has deference over the *golden rule* interpretation[52]. The "Golden rule" would most likely suggest that making one party liable and refusing to make the other liable would defeat the intention of section 130. The problem is that this reasoning/interpretation would have superseded the literal intention of that section, and

---

[52] Nigerian courts have held severally that where words are clear and unambiguous, then statutory provisions should be interpreted accordingly. In *JOSIAH ADETAYO & 2 ORS. V. KUNLE ADEMOLA & ORS*, (2011) 193 LRCN 190 at 217, the court held that: "the Courts must, where the words of an enactment, instrument or other documents are plain, clear and unambiguous, give them or attach to them only such plain, clear, ordinary, unambiguous and natural meanings". The current section 130 provision clearly merely make the first-person liable.

broadened the narrow provision[53]. It would be more reasonable and plain if both parties' acts are **explicitly** incriminated under the provisions of section 130.

The good thing about the Shari'a provisions unlike its counterpart as "Criminal Code Act" is that it envisages the possibility of a same-sex relationship as not being restricted to homosexuality (between males) alone; it covers females as well. However, this development is taken away by the succeeding provision which contains the undertone of restriction of the possibility of commission of the offence to male alone – when it uses "his" alone. Of course, "his" as used here would most likely be interpreted to mean "his and her"[54]. Still, using "his and/or her" where "man and/or woman" as has been used in the same provision would have been more precise.

Lastly, as the other criminal provisions in the Criminal Code Act and the Penal Code Act described above, the subject of sodomy – which is homosexuality or lesbianism in our discussion – is not deemed liable under the Shar'ia law as well. Whether this is what obtains in practice is unclear, but as far as Shar'ia law points, the subject of sodomy is or should not be liable.

---

[53] See: Huffington Post, "Nigeria Gay Trial Disrupted by Thousands of Protesters", Jan. 22, 2014, available at www.huffingtonpost.com/2014/01/22/nigeria-gay-trial-protest_n_4645942.html

[54] It is not unusual to see the "Interpretation section" of Statutes widening the meaning of sex. Such that where "his" is used, same would be implied to cover/imply both sexes

The punishment of the offence in section 131 is rather gruesome, but must be accepted as one of the functions/justifications of punishment[55] – which is to ensure "deterrence" amongst Moslems. It must be noted that unlike the US Constitution, Nigeria does not have a constitutional provision forbidding "cruel and unusual punishment"[56]. Perhaps, if such provision exists in the Constitution, same would have definitely trumped the Shar'ia law provisions, since usually, the Constitution is deemed the supreme law/grundnorm[57].

Section 131 provides that:
"131. Whoever commits the offence of sodomy shall be punished:
*(a) with caning of one hundred lashes **if unmarried**, and shall also be liable to imprisonment for the term of one year, or*
*(b) **if married** with stoning to death (rajm)."*
[Emphasis added]

It is obvious that the section differentiates the punishment for married and unmarried convicts. A reasonable reason for this is the sanctity placed on a relationship as "marriage" under Islamic law[58]. "Adultery" (especially "against the order

---

[55] See: Wright, Valerie (November 2010). *"Evo\nty vs. Severity of Punishment"*. The Sentencing Project. Retrieved 13 October 2012. See also: "Punishment, Justice and International Relations: Ethics and Order After the Cold War", Anthony F. Lang Jr., [Published by: Routledge, Oct 16, 2009]; at page 30

[56] See Article 8 of the US Constitution. It prohibits the Federal Government (and the State via the 14th Amendment) from imposing excessive bail, excessive fines, or **"cruel and unusual punishment"**.

[57] See for example section 1(3) of the Nigerian Constitution, 1999.

[58] A Fatwa explained that: "The Holy Qur'an enjoins the sanctity and

of nature") which could thus contaminate this sanctity is totally abhorred. It would be controversial to suggest that the Ko'ran (as a source of Islamic law) prescribed stoning to death as punishment for adultery. However, it is clear that the Hadith[59] (another source of Islamic law) suggests stoning to death as the punishment for adultery[60]. Thus, if adultery's punishment is stoning to death, stoning to death as punishment for same-sex relationship's or sodomy should be understandable. In summary, a convicted unmarried person would be liable to 100 lashes **plus** (not OR) 1-year imprisonment, while a married person would be liable to stoning to death.

The Same Sex Marriage (Prohibition) Act, 2014
This law is groundbreaking, and revolutionary in some way – mainly as regards what it mainly incriminates – same-sex marriage, and what it further incriminates. We say it is

---

fortitude of conjugal ties." See: http://umma.ws/Fatwa/marriage/
[59] the sayings of Prophet Muhammad [SAW]
[60] [See generally: http://www.thereligionofpeace.com/pages/quran/adultery-stoning.aspx]
Bukhari (6:60:79) – Two people guilty of "illegal" intercourse are brought to Muhammad, who orders them both stoned to death. Apparently their act was out of love, since the verse records the man as trying to shield the woman from the stones.
Bukhari (83:37) – Adultery is one of three justifications for killing a person, according to Muhammad.
Muslim (17:4192) – This hadith clarifies the different penalties for adultery (when the subjects are married), and fornication (when they are not): "in case of married (persons) there is (a punishment) of one hundred lashes and then stoning (to death). And in case of unmarried persons, (the punishment) is one hundred lashes and exile for one year" (See also 17:4191)

revolutionary in some way because the undertone of what it incriminates is already visible in other laws in Nigeria as explained above. The only thing that need be done to those other laws is an amendment to bring them in tune with the intentions of the SSMP[61].

However, it must not be confused, while other laws described above forbids certain acts surrounding LGBTQI, the SSMP mainly forbids marriage between persons of similar sex. Conduct and (marital) status (or efforts to achieve status) are two different concepts. The Nigerian legislature must have relied on and perhaps complacent on the fact that conducts surrounding LGBTQI are already incriminated in the laws described above. Those laws need a proper re-visitation if they must be in-tune with a modern law as the SSMP. The difference between the old criminal provisions and the SSMP can also be discerned from examining the three features of our discussion: sexual orientation, gender identity, and same-sex marriage. The first two features are dealt with by the old criminal provisions discussed above, while the third – same-sex marriage – is dealt with under the SSMP, although reference is being made to the first two features.

As explained above and when juxtaposed with the recommendation chapter in this book, the older criminal law provisions do not fully represent what the SSMP represents. These laws are nothing but relics, which like other relics fail to appreciate new developments in the society. A typical

---

[61] See the Chapter on "Recommendations"

example of an enunciation of this position is the silence of previously discussed law (and even the SSMP) in making provisions for those transgendered or intersex; and even the restriction of persons capable of committing the offences listed to be a male strictly. For the most part, the SSMP prohibits "a **marriage** contract or civil union[62] entered into between persons of same sex, the solemnization of same; and related matters"[63]. For clarification purpose, all the sections of this law would be examined like the previous laws discussed above, since the next part of this article borders on a legal assessment of the SSMP especially. The SSMP is a law aimed at destroying the ultimate aim of lesbians or gays, or even queers wanting to choose a person of their sex as their legal partner – marriage.

Thus, flowing from the Preamble (above) that stated the aim of the Act as prohibiting the status of marriage between persons of similar sex. Section 1 of the Act makes it clear that same-sex marriage is not allowed. Further, perhaps, for persons who have completed a unification process – marriage – prior to the SSMP either in Nigeria or even outside, section 1(b) render such marriage incapable of obtaining the benefits of marriage in Nigeria[64]. Section 2 is where the legislature prescribe what religious bodies must do

---

[62] It must be noted that "marriage" and "civil union" as used in the Act carries different meaning, thus "marriage" is the legal union, "civil union" is wider – see section 7 of the Act, and such acts constituting "civil union" are incriminated as well.
[63] See the Preamble to the law. The related matters are related to rendering such same-sex marriage union void in Nigeria.
[64] See also section 1(2), SSMP Act

– i.e. they must not solemnize or entertain same-sex marriage process; of course, certificates issued in disobedience of this are rendered invalid and would meet the consequence of section 1 described above anyway. Fortunately for the Nigerian government, both Islam and Christianity – the two prominent religions in Nigeria – share the belief that same-sex relationships are forbidden[65]– this conclusion, especially in respect of Christianity, is not uncontroversial, when one consider what is happening in Churches in the West[66] – from where Christianity finds its way to Africa, and Nigeria, through missionaries.

Section 3 of the SSMP reinstate the "normalcy" the Nigerian government considered "marriage". The definition is *blind* to 'developments' of same-sex marital spouses. In section 3 words, only marriages contracted between the classical 'different' sexes are considered marriage. Two questions come to mind. One, what happens to a male who has

---

[65] Whereas the Islamic position has been described above. There are several Biblical provisions condemning same, see for example: in the Old Testament: Leviticus 18:22, Leviticus 20:13; and in the New Testament – 1 Corinthians 6:9-10, Romans 1:26-28, in fact Mark 10:6-9 expressly showed Christianity is in consonance with the Nigerian SSMP. It is not without saying that in support of the LGBTQI movement that Christianity preaches love and same resonates throughout the Bible. There are therefore some other provisions of the Bible that suggest the "accommodation" of those categorized under the LGBTQI in line with Biblical love. See: John 8:7-11, James 4:12, Galatians 5:14, Romans 13: 8-10.

[66] One "All faiths Church" in Florida, USA offers same-sex marriage ceremony to willing couples. See: http://www.inquisitr.com/1749672/florida-churches-are-doing-what-many-county-clerks-refuse-to-do-solemnize-gay-marriages/

undergone a transgender surgery – now making him a female?; now a female, can she marry a man? and vice versa. This is a clear lacuna in section 3 and the SSMP entirely, this issue would be discussed later. The second question is the position of intersex. What is the test for determining if a person belongs to a sex?. The SSMP fails to tell us the *test of sexuality*. The Act must tell us the test of sexuality especially in this epoch of confusion as to sexuality. If the *consensus* suggests that it is the genitalia at birth, then what happens to a Nigerian with two different genitals? are they allowed to marry as well to a consenting partner?, or the government has allowed itself to render life unbearable for certain God creations?. These question must be asked, and answered since the government has made an institution of 'marriage', and the staggering issues embedded as "sexual orientation" and "gender identity" her concern.

Section 4 is the part where Human Right Organizations[67] feel the SSMP threatens citizen's right to Freedom of Association[68] – a right which is, and had been previously guaranteed under section 40 of the Nigerian 1999

---

[67] Especially Human Rights Watch
[68] See: **https://www.hrw.org/news/2014/01/14/nigeria-anti-lgbt-law-threatens-basic-rights**
http://www.hrc.org/blog/nigeria-outlaws-same-sex-marriage-and-lgbt-organizing
http://www.tedxliberdade.com/topic/
http://yubanet.com/world/Nigeria_Anti-Gay_Bill_Threatens_Democratic_Reforms_52100.php#.Vv1lTaQrLlU
http://news.yahoo.com/law-nigeria-bans-same-sex-marriage-220259835.html
http://76crimes.com/2013/06/03/nigeria-ban-on-lawyers-for-gays-all-same-sex-roommates/

Constitution. In subsection 2 of section 4, PDAs[69] — having same-sex as its rational — are also incriminated where they are expressed directly or indirectly[70]. Prohibiting "indirect" PDA for example by words spoken must be accepted as trampling upon "freedom of expression/speech" — which is, and had already been guaranteed by section 39 of the Nigerian 1999 Constitution. The question must be asked in this respect (in the next part of this article) whether the Nigerian government (via her legislature) can restrict the exercise of these rights by her citizens. Also, especially if the SSMP is a response justified under section 45 of the constitution on protecting public morals in the Nigerian society.

Section 5 is the controlling section of the SSMP Act, it clearly defines what constitutes an offence under the Act — thereby meeting the requirements of section 36(12) of the Nigerian 1999 Constitution, which stipulates that a crime must be defined. Clearly, subsection 1 of section 5 explicitly makes civil union and marriage contract between persons of the same sex illicit, and punishable with 14 years imprisonment. As mentioned earlier, it is important to note the definition of "civil union" in section 7 — Interpretation section of the Act — the definition is wide and it includes importantly "significant relationship". The question that easily comes to mind is whether the Nigerian government should interfere into the "family life" between two

---

[69] Public Display of Affection
[70] See a somewhat similar provision in section 217 of Criminal Code Act, which incriminates "gross indecency", but between males.

consenting adults, and whether the government can make herself the *gatekeeper* of sex or identity or marriage.

In subsection 2, the provisions of section 4(1) and (2) (on registering/maintaining/participating/operating gay societies, groups, clubs or societies; and persons of same sex exhibiting PDAs in public) are greeted with their punishments – 10 years imprisonment. This provision likewise is a direct blow to the *right to freedom of association* mentioned above.

For easy comprehension, it is better to *divide* the last subsection – subsection 3 – of section 5. In its first part, persons who administer, witnesses, abets or aids the solemnization of same-sex marriage or union are liable to imprisonment for 10 years. The problem with this provision is that this provision is targeted at Pastors, Ministers, Clerics – Christian or Moslem. Should the government interfere, regulate or prescribe what people who preside at religious gatherings do?; won't this amount to meddling politics/government with religion?. These are the questions. There are those who believe that there would be a better justification for the government to interfere with religion and its practice in Nigerian churches or mosques religious centres are being asked to pay taxes on monies they collect from their congregation.

The case of the House of Rainbow Church in Lagos – whose religious leader[71] (accommodating persons falling

---

[71] Pastor Rowland Jide Macaulay

under the LGBTQI) was forced to leave Nigeria[72] after which the church itself was destroyed is instructive in this regard. Are religious practices void of injuring a third party really the concern of the government, in Nigeria? to pro-gay rights activists, these are the questions the Nigerian government via her legislature perhaps has not seem to ask or address. As held by this author, the ordinary perception is that religious leaders are entrusted with the interpretation of their religion; but can the government interpret their religion on their behalf, and make what they (might) consider to be within their religion a crime?

The second part of subsection 3 is the part that incriminates the acts of persons "supporting" the registration, operation, and sustenance of gay clubs, societies, organizations, processions or meetings in Nigeria. As one would think, anyone who supports the sustenance of a gay or more widely the LGBTQI community must have first supported the course of being gay or the LGBTQI movement. So, it would be reasonable to imply the wide implications of this part of subsection 3. We are yet to see the operation of this section, and its operation concerns persons as this writer as a lawyer.

In addition, a fluid interpretation of this section is that if a lawyer represents a consortium of clients who are gays, in a Nigerian court, agitating, supporting, and arguing for the right to freedom of association of the group, then the lawyer would be liable under the SSMP for "supporting" gay

---

[72] http://www.theparadigmng.com/2014/01/18/nigerian-gay-pastor-rev-rowland-on-the-run-relocate-to-the-uk/

societies. This is a reasonable interpretation since the Act has failed to examine the consequence(s) of using the word "supporting" largely, and has also failed to define what "support" means or provide exceptions to what constitute "support".

Right after the SSMP Act was promulgated, the UN via UNAIDS and Global Funds have expressed "support" for the gay community, and have even requested that the Nigerian government reconsider the law[73], why are these bodies not prosecuted?. This only shows the lack of consideration of the invocation of the SSMP in a country as Nigeria. It appears Nigeria wants to accept all forms of "developments" from international organizations she's a party to but has chosen to employ a 'filter' so that certain developments and necessary accommodations are shut out. While it is not bad to employ a 'filter', the following part of the article challenges a law as SSMP, and questions its validity/existence amongst other existing laws in Nigeria.

---

[73] http://www.aidspan.org/gfo_article/global-fund-and-unaids-urge-nigeria-reconsider-new-anti-gay-law

CHAPTER 3

"...the 'hypocrisy' complained of resides in the fact that: "how can we incriminate a relationship because it has the propensity of leading to human extinction/barrenness when the people clamouring for this type of relationship are a minority?"

-gbenga Odugbemi

<u>An Assessment of Laws on Same-Sex Relationship in Nigeria</u>

i. *Assessment/Reviews*

This part puts the relevant provisions on same-sex marriage as it relates to sexual orientation and gender identity as it operates in Nigeria, particularly, the SSMP on a scale with other laws which predates the SSMP. By 'laws', we mean the Nigerian 1999 Constitution, and such relevant international legislation Nigeria is committed to or has domesticated. As mentioned in the early part of this work, this exercise is not meant to suggest 'support' of what the SSMP incriminates or otherwise; instead, it only tries to exhibit whether the SSMP and other relevant laws could be said to capable of 'co-existing' considering other pre-existing laws, and Nigeria's international commitments. If the "SSMP and its cohorts" (the Criminal Code Act, the Penal Code [Northern Nigeria] Act, and the Shari'a law) survive the assessment construing existing laws (fundamental rights), then the former must be truly accepted as *"good or just law"*[74] in the Nigeria society. If on the other hand, the reverse is the case, this article only

---

[74] Flowing from the idea of "Lex iniusta non est lex" – an unjust law is no law at all

calls for a *re-visitation* by the Nigerian legislature, so the SSMP and its cohorts can have true "*legal and just*" colour.

Fortunately, aside maybe two or three other issues, the majority of arguments the SSMP and its cohorts are exposed to are "rights or freedom – oriented". This implies that the several rights of persons whose status/activities are now being incriminated were already pre-guaranteed by several laws in Nigeria. Such relevant laws to which reference would be made includes: locally, the Nigerian 1999 Constitution, internationally, but domestically: the African Charter on Human and Peoples' Right[75] (hereinafter referred to as the 'African Charter'), Universal Declaration of Human Right[76], The International Covenant on Civil and Political Rights[77],

---

[75] Also referred to as the "Banjul Charter", 1982. Nigeria domesticated the African Charter by virtue of her section 12, 1999 Constitution when the legislature promulgated "African Charter on Human and Peoples' Rights (Ratification and Enforcement) Act" in 1983.

[76] 1948. It must be noted that the UDHR lacks legal binding effect (see: the "legal Character" of the UDHR in **http://www.ohchr.org/EN/Issues/SRHRDefenders/Pages/Declaratio n.aspx**). However, Nigeria has integrated the provisions of the UDHR because of the United Nations general assembly resolution 48/138 of December 1993 which enjoined member states (including Nigeria, since 1960) to establish and strengthen national institutions for the promotion and protection of human rights and fundamental freedom in their countries. The Nigerian Legislature established the National Human Rights Commission via the National Human Rights Commission Act, 1995. That commission has its purpose to foster the provisions of the UDHR in Nigeria. (See: http://www.nigeriarights.gov.ng/UniversalDeclaration.php)

[77] 1966. Unlike the UDHR, the ICCPR has legal binding effect, and was ratified by Nigeria in 1993.

and lastly, the International Covenant on Economic, Social and Cultural Rights[78].

The confluence of these legislative provisions above is that people, everyone, equally have some basic rights or freedoms. Such rights include (in relation to our discussion): the right to freedom from discrimination (base on sex, gender), right to privacy, family life, conscience, belief; right to freedom of religion, the right to freedom of association, and importantly, right to freedom of expression/speech. While it is undisputed that these basic rights are within these legislations and operable (or ought to be operable) in Nigeria. The next question is: "can gays, lesbians, bisexuals, transgendered persons, queers, intersex be beneficiaries of these rights or is there a filter?". In other words, can the Nigerian government approbate – give these rights with one hand – and then reprobate – take it away with the other hand via the SSMP and its cohorts. This discussion shall unfold in the following discussions of the relevant rights.

Right to Freedom from Discrimination

This right provides the bed-rock for all the agitations of the LGBTQI community – that despite the fact that they are a minority (in the Nigerian society), that they shouldn't be discriminated against based on their sex and/or gender. As shall be seen, this agitation has a firm standing in several

---

[78] 1976, ratified by Nigeria on the same day as the ICCPR – 29th July, 1993. The ICESCR is legally binding, see: **https://www.escr-net.org/resources/section-5-background-information-icescr**

laws, although the SSMP and it cohorts might seem to be *blinded* to their existence.

If there are one thing laws often tries to achieve, it is *equality* in all ramifications, although same cannot be said of some of the Nigerian criminal laws as discussed above. By ensuring freedom from discrimination, the laws on the issue tries to portray *equality* amongst the Nigerian people. The understanding of this right can be easily understood from the understanding of the *Mischief rule* used in the interpretation of statutes and rules, especially as it relates to "circumstances of birth" or "sex" as determinant factors for inheritance in Nigerian.

In Nigeria, under intestacy rule[79], it used to be that if a child is born outside wedlock, such child cannot be a beneficiary of his married parents' inheritance, because of the sole reason – circumstances of his/her birth, which is "birth outside wedlock". Also, some cultures or customary rules hold that a female cannot ordinarily take/inherit from his biological parent, even if the deceased make the female child a direct beneficiary under his/her will. Under such

---

[79] "Intestacy" means a deceased person died without a will. It is the opposite of "testacy", if a person died testate, it means he had a will before he died. The implication of having a will or not after dying is that, under testacy, the wishes of the deceased as described in his will applies to his estate/property disposition. In contrast, where he dies intestate (without will), the court steps in, and distribute his property in accordance with the intestacy rules – it is rule describing the hierarchy of who should take part of the deceased estate, it usually starts from the deceased's spouse, to his children, then parents etc.

customary rules, only a male child can inherit. However, with the advent of the right to freedom from discrimination in the Nigerian 1999 Constitution, grounds as "circumstances of birth" or "sex" cannot be used to refuse a person inheritance again, because the law forbids discrimination to entitlements or benefits on such grounds[80], and there are other grounds too, as race, ethnic group etc. In applying the "Mischief rule" of interpretation, one of the question the court ask is: "what is the mischief which the new law has come to correct?". In the Will/Estate exposition given above, the mischief would be: "people are being denied inheritance based on their sex or circumstance of birth". The new law – section 42 of the Nigerian 1999 Constitution – has thus come correct that mischief and the latter law would apply. The question then beckons, "how can we have a new law that discriminates or refuse a person the benefits of marriage in Nigeria because of his sex or gender? even with the continued existence of section 42 of the Nigerian Constitution.

What we are trying to say is that the law considers as equal, every person even if they come out to say I belong to this gender or otherwise. If we agree that there are just two sexes – male and female; if a person says he is female, section 42 says treat him equally as you do a female, if he says he is

---

[80] One of the test such customary law need to pass before it enjoys application in a Nigerian court is that it is not contrary to an existing law in Nigeria. Thus, since the Constitution in section 42 would directly refute such customary law idea, it follows automatically that such customary law/rule is inapplicable, and thus any person, regardless of the circumstances of their birth or sex can thus inherit.

male, treat him equally as a male – enjoyment of marriage benefits inclusive. The law looks at the **existence** of belonging to a gender, not belonging to a **particular** gender to determine equality. A person's personal right to choose which of the gender or sex he or she belongs to does not and should not thus affect the applicability of the right.

The right to freedom from discrimination is 'dormant' in nature when compared to other rights. It puts a duty on the government's part. It becomes 'responsive' when the government fails to avoid discrimination based on the several factors – as age, sex, gender, political opinion, religion, circumstances of birth etc.

However, it must be noted that contrary to notorious belief amongst the LGBTQI movement, the provisions of section 42(1) of the Nigerian 1999 Constitution is not a proper basis to assume the illegality of the SSMP and/or its cohorts as regards the "sexual orientation", "gender identity", or "same-sex marriage" of persons. We say this for two reasons. Clearly, section 42(1) provides thus:

*42. (1) A citizen of Nigeria of a particular community, ethnic group, place of origin, **sex**, religion or political opinion shall **NOT**, by reason only that he is such a person:-*

(a) be subjected either expressly by, or in the practical application of, any law in force in Nigeria or any executive or administrative action of the government, to disabilities or restrictions to which citizens of Nigeria of other communities, ethnic groups, places of origin, sex, religions or political opinions are not made subject; or

[Emphasis added]

A proper reading of this provision would reflect that what the constitution forbids is giving preference or special treatment to a person base on any of the operating factors[81] (in our discussion "sex"[82]), where the same preference or special treatment is not given to similar persons in "another part of Nigeria". The controlling phrase being "another part of Nigeria". So, if A – a female is allowed to inherit property – in the South-Western part of Nigeria, B (also a female in the Northern part of Nigeria) must be allowed to so inherit as well – this is the intention of section 42. What the constitution forbids is where B is restricted from inheriting in the North when females as B are allowed to so inherit in the South Western part.

It, therefore, follows that if there's a law making same-sex union illegal (as the SSMP) in a part of Nigeria, a person cannot complain of discrimination if he/she is subject to the same treatment under the law in another part of Nigeria. It is even more interesting and true since the SSMP is an Act of the Federal Government of Nigeria – thereby enjoying operation all over the country. Thus, since the Act forbids same-sex union in all parts of Nigeria, a person cannot complain of discrimination based on his/her sex or gender. The reverse would have been the case if same-sex union is allowed in State A and disallowed in State B in Nigeria; then, the concerned parties in State B would be able to invoke the provisions of section 42. Females are allowed to inherit as

---

[81] *community, ethnic group, place of origin, **sex**, religion or political opinion*
[82] Note that 'gender' is not mentioned as a factor in section 42, and a 'catch-all' phrase as 'other factors' is not used.

do males (by virtue of section 42) under estate rules discussed above in relation to customary laws which forbids females because females are so allowed to inherit in other parts of Nigeria. It is because females are so allowed in other parts of Nigeria, that they are said to be allowed in the other parts too, regardless of customary laws/rules in such places.

The summary is that the constitutional provision on discrimination does not say it is impossible to discriminate generally based on the factors listed. What it is saying, in essence, is that, if based on the listed factors, some people in Nigeria are accorded a treatment, same type of people will not be refused similar treatment based on similar factors in other parts of Nigeria. The case brought by Joseph Teriah Ebah at the Federal High Court in Abuja FCT would have been instructive in further explaining the provisions of section 42 on the discrimination issue. However, since the case has been thrown out, for lack of locus standi by the plaintiff[83], this expectation has been short-lived[84]. The validity of the court's ruling in throwing the case out is well-received when in the words of the plaintiff, he confirms that "he decided to sue even though he is not LGBT because *'I decided I wasn't going to accept a Nigeria that was discriminatory.'* Although the plaintiff made mention of 'discrimination' in

---

[83] The Court was of the opinion that plaintiff not being gay or a person who could be categorized under the LGBTQI community lacks the standing necessary to bring the case before it, since the outcome of the case won't have any effect whatsoever on the plaintiff anyway.

[84] http://www.buzzfeed.com/lesterfeder/nigerian-court-throws-out-challenge-to-anti-lgbt-law#.qs1B4xRao

his words, it's unclear whether section 42 of the Nigerian 1999 Constitution is a basis used in his pleadings. Whichever way, LGBTQI rights to freedom from discrimination cannot properly be challenged based on the said section 42. A viable basis is discussed below.

Another pertinent reason why section 42 is not a good basis is because even if we agree that SSMP is discriminatory based on that section, section 42 would only be a good basis to the extent that it forbids discrimination based ONLY on "sex". Section 42 do not use the word "gender"[85]. The LGBTQI course or movement entails not just "sexual orientation", but inclusively, **gender** identity". Now, it might be possible to argue that the *ejusdem generis* rule would validate the import of "gender" in the operating factors listed in section 42. However, it is also possible to argue that the legislature meant a "restriction" when it didn't include "gender"; this is true since a literal meaning is always given preference over other rules of interpretation. A "Golden rule" interpretation might also be applied in support of the former argument – *ejusdem generis* rule – so as to prevent the provisions of section 42 from an *absurd* interpretation which

---

[85] There is a great difference between 'sex' and 'gender' especially when it comes to LGBTQI issues. In general terms, "sex" refers to the biological differences between males and females, such as the genitalia and genetic differences. "Gender" is more difficult to define but can refer to the role of a male or female in society (gender role), or an individual's concept of themselves (gender identity). [see: http://www.medicalnewstoday.com/articles/232363.php]. "Sex" would refer to cases of persons as gays/homosexuals, lesbians, or bisexuals, but "gender" would refer to "transgender" persons.

might result if discrimination is prevented base on sex but not on gender. Lastly, and more controversially, in this regard, it might also be argued that the import of "gender" is totally "shut out" in section 42 since it did not contain the phrase/general word, which ordinarily gives life to the *"ejusdem generis"* rule.

In *Walling v. Peavy-Wilson Lumber Co.*[86], the court held in respect of the rule that: where "**general words** follow enumerations of particular classes or persons or things, the general words shall be construed as applicable only to persons or things of the same general nature or kind as those enumerated." The controlling word in this dicta is "general words", an example of such "general words" is when a statutory provision lists: "cats, dogs, fowls and **other animals**". "Other animals" is the "general word" that follows the enumerations of certain type of animals referred to, thus for the operation of *"ejusdem generis"* rule, a lion, tiger or other wild animal would not fit in the "other animals", but rabbit, sheep or goat would fit in. Bringing this explanation to the provisions of section 42, the Constitution refuse to use any "general word" after enumerating likely discriminatory factors. This, of course, is an anomaly, considering the fact that basis for discrimination is likely to develop with time as currently in today's Nigeria; "general words" could have being employed to cater for this situation in section 42.

Fortunately, the provisions of other relevant international organizations statutes are radical in all of the unsuitability of

---

[86] 49 F. Supp. 846, 859 (W.D. La. 1943)

section 42 of the Nigerian Constitution to challenge the SSMP and its cohorts. In respect of the last discussion on the use of "general words", the African Charter unlike the provisions of section 42 used "general words" at the end of the enumerated basis of discrimination. Thus, an import of "gender" as a basis would be plausible, since it flows with the specifically listed basis/factors. The African Charter used "or any status"[87] This same trend is repeated as regards the UDHR[88], ICCPR[89], ICESCR[90]. Also, as regards the fortification on whether similar treatment is operable in other parts of Nigeria, the provisions of this other international organizations is clearer as compared to section 42. For example, more closely, the African Charter in Article 2 provides that:

"**Every individual shall be entitled to the enjoyment of the rights and freedoms recognized and guaranteed in the present Charter** *without distinction of any kind such as race, ethnic group, colour, sex, language, religion, political or any other opinion, national and social origin, fortune, birth or any status.*"
[Emphasis added]

There is no *rampart* as to whether similar treatment is given in other parts or otherwise, the African Charter and other similar provision are direct, and that is that everyone is entitled to the basic rights contained in the instrument. The next question is whether the rights attacked by the SSMP and its cohorts are contained in an instrument as the African

---

[87] See Art. 2
[88] See Art. 2, it uses "or other status"
[89] See Art. 2, it uses "or other opinion" and "or other status"
[90] See Art. 2, it uses "or other opinion" and "or other status"

Charter. The two basic threatened rights are right to life (which is guaranteed under Art. 4), and the right to freedom of association (guaranteed under Art. 10). Without making unnecessary repetitions, similar provisions resonated throughout the ICCPR, ICESR and the UDHR as well. It must thus be agreed that while it is quite unfortunate that section 42 of the Nigerian 1999 Constitution can't be a (proper) basis to properly challenge the SSMP and its cohorts, international organization's legislations some of which Nigeria has even domesticated are the proper basis, the African Charter especially.

To this extent, however, it is fairly reasonable to say the SSMP and its cohorts' provisions are not *within* these laws. In other words, the SSMP and its cohorts are discriminatory, based on gender and/or sex. The discrimination is that certain persons who have sexual attractions to persons of their sex are prevented from expressing such sexual attraction, and are prevented from marrying each other.

Right to Privacy and Family Life

The right to privacy is guaranteed under section 37 of the Nigerian 1999 Constitution, but not well described as did the UDHR and the ICCPR in their Article 12 and 17 respectively. The latter, for example, provides that:

*"No one shall be subjected to arbitrary or unlawful interference with his **privacy**, **family**, home or correspondence, nor to unlawful attacks on his honour and reputation."*
[Emphasis added]

A contradicting section to this provision in the SSMP is its section 1(1) that incriminates same-sex union. The argument is that a law interfering into what constitutes 'marriage' – which has the potential of resulting in a 'family' is unconstitutional. Added is the fact that the desire of persons of similar sex to enter into such union is private, and the government (including through its laws) should respect that. One important question that frequently comes up in discussions as regards persons of same-sex getting married and the "family" argument is that they can't reproduce, and therefore couldn't raise a family. Consequently, that the "right to family" argument cannot be used to support their freedom. In fact, the impossibility of reproduction and the imminent phobia of human extinction operates as one of the reasons the Gambian President has refused to legalize homosexuality in The Gambia[91]. Although, while we must concede that these arguments are valid, i.e. that person of similar sex in a union cannot reproduce, these arguments are not without flaws. There are four possible arguments to rebut the arguments.

One, examine this scenario. In most legal jurisprudence, "self-defense/justification" is allowed when there's an imminent danger on one's person (the subject) or someone related/connected to the subject. If A aims a gun at B (C's daughter) so he can kill her, if C retaliated faster with a

---

[91] "Homosexuality will never be tolerated and in fact will attract the ultimate penalty since it is intended to bring humanity to an inglorious extinction" – The Gambia President, Yahya Jammeh. See: http://www.slate.com/blogs/outward/2014/02/24/gambian_president_calls_gays_ungodly_vermin_how_america_should_respond.html

gunshot that killed A, C's act would be considered 'self-defense' or justified, since A was going to use a deadly weapon on B, C also is allowed to use a deadly weapon. The question is: "can we say because self-defense is allowed, then most people would most likely die?". The reasoning of the law is allowing the freedom to defend oneself (primary concern), the consequence, whether a person would defend himself or otherwise is different (secondary concern). The same argument resonates in the same-sex union arguments – that allowing persons of same-sex engage in their union would lead to that society's human extinction or that it's not familial is a secondary issue. The argument here is not that law should not take consequences of freedoms/rights into consideration, what we are saying is that in this regard – in the Nigerian situation, such secondary argument is hypocritical. Even if we agree that The Gambia might go into extinction if that country allows a same-sex union, her population is below 2 million; Nigeria's population is almost 180 million – so such fear in the Nigerian context is without merit.

Secondly and flowing from the above discussion, the 'hypocrisy' complained of resides in the fact that: "how can we incriminate a relationship because it has the propensity of leading to human extinction when the people clamouring for this type of relationship are a minority?". The gay population in Nigeria cannot be up to 10% because the majority of Nigerians holds the belief of being heterosexual anyway, and are heterosexual. The larger percentage who are heterosexual will continue to reproduce, and the phobia of human extinction could be allayed.

Thirdly, what is a family? the definition of a family does not necessary has to contain a child(-ren). It would suffice that from the common definition of what a family is, that a group of persons related by marriage alone would be sufficient to constitute same. "Giving birth" is just another factor that could stand as a basis for a familial relationship. If not, what would the society term a couple (this time a man and a woman) living together without a child? – either by their own agreement not to reproduce or perhaps by medical complications?. Is the couple still not a family (even if they do not have a child)? are these type of (heterosexual) couples not constituting to human extinction?. If we answer these questions in the affirmative, then, we must accept that a couple – either of similar sex or different sex is sufficient to constitute a family – even without a child.

Lastly, there are adoption provisions, even in Nigeria, a gay couple may adopt children and look after them, in fact, reports shows that gay couples have a higher tendency of being the best parents[92]. Succinctly put, there's no way allowing same-sex relationship is attacking human existence, also, a marital relationship either between persons of the same sex or otherwise is sufficient for the definition of "family", and that's what the constitution tries to protect. Hence, the provision of section 1(1) of the SSMP lacks merit

---

[92] See: http://www.livescience.com/17913-advantages-gay-parents.html

when it attacks the "privacy" and the familial sanctity protected by the relevant provisions mentioned earlier.

However, rather sadly, we must not forget that the provisions of section 45 of the Nigerian Constitution, that provision allows the government through the legislature to restrict the exercise of certain rights – right to privacy inclusive. So, it is possible, and it could be argued that the emancipation of the SSMP is an upshot of the exercise of that power in the said provision. Conclusively, whereas the provisions on right to privacy/family life are being attacked by the SSMP and its cohorts, the Nigerian government can regulate the privacy and family life of persons in Nigeria (at least) because of section 45, so the SSMP and its cohorts pass this assessment in this respect.

Right to Freedom of Religion
The question about same-sex relationship or its union and religion challenges the State whether it can be the 'gatekeeper' of religious practices. The SSMP in its section 2(1) prescribes or at least interferes into what religious bodies – churches or mosques can do in their place of worship. It provides:

"A marriage contract or civil union entered into between persons of same sex **shall not be solemnized in a church, mosque or any other place of worship in Nigeria."**
[Emphasis added]

The State through her legislature has constituted herself as the concierge of religious practices. Even if the relevance of section 10 of the Nigerian 1999 Constitution is not challenging enough, we must cite the provisions of section 38. It provides:

"Every person shall be entitled to freedom of thought, conscience, and religion, including freedom to change his religion or belief, **and freedom** *(either alone or in community with others and in public or in private)* **to manifest and propagate his religion or belief in worship, teaching, practice and observance."**
[Emphasis added]

For similar provisions of section 38, see Article 18 of the UDHR and ICCPR. The controlling phrase in these provisions is the freedom to manifest and propagate practice of one's religion.

Here, we ask, "if there are several laws including section 38 of the Constitution providing that persons (including ministers in churches or mosques) have freedom to practice their religion, how do we interpret section 2(1) of the SSMP?". Clearly, the latter section was made without consideration of other relevant provisions in respect of freedom to practice religion. If certain minister of churches or mosques finds solemnizing same-sex couple's union as being within the tenets of their religion, it appears section 38 (unrestricted as it seems) would allow this.

Unfortunately, just as section 37 discussed above, the current section 38 is also not an absolute right in the Nigerian context. The State (the Nigeria government) has the right and duty to restrict the exercise of certain rights (including as regards religious practices) by virtue of section 45 of the Constitution. It's reasonable to believe the government has a concern for "public morality" – a 'concern' validated by section 45, and that is the essence of the SSMP and its cohorts. Truly, the religious practices in the society should be checked by the State. Even in the US, in *Reynolds vs. US*[93], the court was of the opinion that since polygamy is not legal in the US, a religion permitting same could be restricted. Since allowing the 'free-ride' of the religion practice would mean that the law forbidding polygamy would be useless. Also, a religion that permits human sacrifice might agitate for a similar 'free-ride' to take citizens and use them for sacrifice, hence, the need for a leash on the neck of religious practices. So, should the Islamic or Christianity religion or any religion in Nigeria permits same-sex union, the Nigerian government can argue that it wishes to control the practice of such religion because of her duty to maintain *public morality* amongst the Nigerian people.

Arguments refuting the Nigerian government's power to review religious practices cannot be correctly substantiated in law. Most countries in the West do similar. As stated above, a religion worshipper cannot say because his religion requires and permits him to offer children as a human

---

[93] *REYNOLDS V. UNITED STATES*, 98 U.S. (8 Otto.) 145 (1878)

sacrifice, then, that the State should allow him to practice his religion and kill people. However, the difference in the exercise of the restriction on religious practices as do Nigeria currently and what obtains in the more developed country must be differentiated. Too often, in latter countries, when a restriction is created as regards a religious practice, the practice usually perhaps affects another person's life, threatens their property, or have the consequence of having some type of damage to a third party. Whichever way, the consensus in such instances is such that the restriction should be validated as regards the religious practice.

Luckily, in more developed countries, and in Nigeria, there's secularism of religion, so it is hard for a religion to agitate for the consensus of its practice. It leaves room for the government to decide which of the practice which affects a third-party's right should be restricted – as often said, A might have a right, but where A's right ends is where B's right starts. An ideal way to determine if the same-sex union or what the other laws on this issue incriminate would have been to carry out a poll and get the consensus of people as regards the issue, whether same should be incriminated or otherwise. But, the response to such poll in the Nigerian setting is already known[94], one thing that is, however, certain is that, such response would be based on no reason in law or other viable basis, but rather on each person's belief of what they think is morally or religiously or culturally right. Truly,

---

[94] Most likely, most Nigerians would argue for the ban of same-sex union in churches/mosques. A larger percentage of the population currently abhors the LGBTQI movement.

what the interpretation of section 38 and 45 of the Nigerian Constitution would then mean is that the right to religion respects beliefs and opinions of the people, but not entirely with the practice, the government can interfere with the practices of the religion.

In surmise, the argument here is that same-sex marriage or other issues embedded in the LGBTQI movement have no way of affecting a third party. In fact, parties involved in the issues embedded do so by consent, and the effect of the activities involved are solely on the parties involved, the activities do not spill or affect any third party in any way. This is the reason the exercise of the Nigerian government's power in restricting the practice of religion in churches and mosques in this regard is questionable, although legal.

Another argument in support of the Nigerian government's position as regards the validity of the SSMP in Nigeria as it relates to the exercise of religion is the provisions of Article 8 of the African Charter on freedom of religion – which Nigeria has domesticated. Article 8 provides:
"Freedom of conscience, the profession and free practice of religion shall be guaranteed. No one may, **subject to law and order***, be submitted to measures restricting the exercise of these freedoms."*
[Emphasis added]
The phrase "subject to law and order" [just as section 45 mentioned above] must be interpreted as making the exercise of the freedom of religion practice subject to existing laws. One of such existing law is the SSMP and its section 2(1).

No doubt, while the Islamic religion seems to totally forbid solemnizing gay unions, there is an ongoing difference in arguments amongst churches as to whether such solemnization is biblical or otherwise in the Christianity realm. In fact, as at when this book is written, a Church of England Bishop (Nicholas Chamberlain) came out and confirmed he is gay and in a gay relationship[95]. However, since this author is not an authority on the Christianity religion, it would be safe to rely on the current trend. The current trend is such that in the West, some churches allow same-sex union solemnization and ceremonies in their churches. Anglican and Episcopal churches[96] seem to allow it with some restrictions – depending on the country[97]. The now extinct gay church in Nigeria – House of Rainbow – would seem to allow such solemnization of course – since disallowing it directly counter what the church stands for.

At the end, we can say Christianity tends to create *room* for the allowance of solemnizing gay marriages, while the Islamic religion totally forbids it. At least, to the best of this author's knowledge, there have been no mosque solemnizing persons belonging to the LGBTQI community. While the Islamic position has thus demonstrated coherence and

---

[95] http://www.bbc.com/news/uk-politics-37257005
[96] https://www.washingtonpost.com/news/acts-of-faith/wp/2015/07/01/why-the-episcopal-church-is-still-debating-gay-marriage/
[97] See also: http://www.inquisitr.com/1749672/florida-churches-are-doing-what-many-county-clerks-refuse-to-do-solemnize-gay-marriages/

consistency all over the world, its counterpart – Christianity – has not.

As radical as it would seem, the quest for allowing same-sex solemnization in Nigerian churches should be advocated by Nigerian church ministers, owing to the idea that Christianity was **introduced** to Africa, and Nigeria specifically (in the 15th century). The idea of the "introduction" should ordinarily suggest obedience and followership of the Christianity religious practices, including evolving practices. Thus, if those who introduce the religion are suggesting allowing the solemnization of gay couples in churches, why won't the receivers accept or follow? The question is controversial, but while we look at the controversy, we must remember the *passage* of the Christianity religion into Nigeria. One of the first Christian mission (perhaps, the first) in Nigeria built in Badagry, Lagos by Henry Townsend was of the Church of England. Today, the Archbishop of Canterbury (Church of England) who appointed Nicholas Chamberlain referred to above confirmed he knew the latter is gay before appointing him as a Bishop. He added, and this is the point of note: *"…his appointment as bishop of Grantham was made on the basis of his skills and calling to serve the Church in the Diocese of Lincoln…he lives within the bishops' guidelines and his sexuality is completely irrelevant to his office."* The early church which was the *conduit* for Christianity into Nigeria supports the LGBTQI movement[98], what exactly is the excuse of Nigerian Churches?

---

[98] One might argue, it only supports "gay", but no, such argument is flawed, the Church can't support gay and isolate the remaining

A while back, when this author was in London, and I believe Nigerians who have lived in Nigeria and London, UK would attest to this. I notice the streets are always filled with Nigerians on Sundays. Everyone (Christians of course) is all dressed and trolling into every church they could find; whereas the British (those who introduced Christianity to Nigerians) just sit down at home, or go to church (dressed in whatever they could find) and spend few hours there. This author is not castigating the attitude of Nigerian Christians in diaspora, especially in London. However, it seems to this author that it is quite humorous and ironic how Nigerians are the ones trying to *give back* the Christianity religion to the English people, so much that a man was forced to leave a London bus recently for instigating a sermon and preaching while riding in it. The issues here are very controversial. So, we have Nigeria trying to give, teach, and force the English – those who introduced her to the religion (Christianity) back to Christianity. We also have those introducing the religion suggesting that gay unions are within the religion's practices, but clearly, the Nigerian Christians have refused to agree with this.

Aside all of the above, the provisions of section 45 of the Nigerian Constitution is still very much relevant in the Nigerian case. Thus, on the issue of freedom to practice religion and the legal restriction, it is clear that while other laws as UDHR and ICCPR envisages an absolute freedom to exercise religious practices as one fits, the Nigerian 1999 Constitution and the African Charter clearly place some

---

sexuality/gender identities, especially since the Archbishop confirms that sexuality do not affect office.

restrictions. Whether the position of the latter must be accepted as 'good law' is another issue entirely. However, to be candid, on the validity of section 2(1) of the SSMP, it does seem that the Nigerian legislature has a valid legal basis for such provision.

Right to Freedom of Association
This right received its 'attack' from the provisions of section 4 of the SSMP. Thus, in further bolstering the position and the purpose of the SSMP in its preamble, the Act finds it important to also prohibit the existence of gay associations and what they do. Section 4 provides:

"The registration of gay clubs, societies and organizations, their sustenance, processions and meetings **is prohibited."**
[Emphasis added]

A proper reading of this section would show that prohibition of "sustenance" as used represents a 'blow' not only to the gay community but also to the supporters of gay club as an association – who might not be gay themselves – but who wants to see the gay community achieve a place in the Nigerian society. The assessment is on how this section can co-exist with an already existing section – section 40 of the Nigerian 1999 Constitution. That section provides that:
"Every person shall be entitled to assemble **freely and associate with other persons,** *and in particular, he may form or belong to any political party, trade union or any other association* **for the protection of his interests…"**
[Emphasis added]

Nothing more can be clearer than this provision as regards the support the constitution envisaged for persons to be able to form an association with aim as 'fostering the interest of its members'. It is, of course, clear that no such professed association currently exist in Nigeria mainly because of the operation of the SSMP. However, prior to the SSMP, the House of Rainbow Church mentioned earlier would suffice as an association aimed at fostering LGBTQI relationships. Are these type of associations a mere exercise of the freedom of association assured by section 40? In the Nigerian context, the answer is an upshot of when the association exists/existed.

Prior to the SSMP in 2014, such association would have been licit and representing the exercise of freedom of association of its members. However, with the advent of the SSMP in 2014 hitherto, such association would be considered illegal, not just because the SSMP makes it so. It is also because the Nigerian 1999 Constitution that gives the right to association refuse to make it absolute when it decorates the State with powers to restrict the exercise of the freedom to association when it considers such exercise as attacking *public morality*. As other previous rights discussed above, it would seem that a valid argument for the Nigerian government is that the SSMP and its attack on the freedom of association is an exhibition of its powers in section 45 of the Nigerian Constitution. The discussion here, therefore, adopts the questionable nature of the Nigerian government in exercising this power under section 45 in this manner. In a developed society, and I believe in Nigeria – as a developing country – laws should be made with reasons. As far as the majority of the Nigerian populace is concerned, the rationale behind the SSMP and its supportive laws are without proper reason.

In further support of the Nigerian government position, Article 10 of the African Charter supports the provisions of section 40 and 45 of the 1999 Constitution. It states:
"Every individual shall have the right to free association **provided that he abides by the law.***"*
[Emphasis added]

An example of such law is the SSMP since that law restricts an association that fosters gay relationships, such association's continued existence must be resolved as illegal in the Nigerian context, at least. However, it must be cited that a similar provision in the UDHR as regards the right to freedom of association of persons is unrestricted as do the latter provisions. Importantly, Article 20 of the UDHR provides that: *"Everyone has the right to freedom of peaceful assembly and association".* This provision contains no condition just as Article 22 of the ICCPR, which provides: *"Everyone shall have the right to freedom of association with others..."*

Like the previous right discussed above, it must be resolved that although construing the provisions of the UDHR and the ICCPR, it would constitute an infringement of the freedom to association of gays to prohibit their association. However, more closely, the African Charter and the Nigerian Constitution supports and provides a basis for the 'prohibition'. So, the Nigerian government *pass* this assessment as well.

Right to Freedom of Expression
Flowing from the attack to "freedom of association" discussed above, inclusively, by prohibiting the 'meetings' of gays by the same section of the SSMP, the freedom to expression as promised in section 39[99] of the Nigerian 1999 Constitution is also attacked. It could be resolved that a 'meeting' would necessarily be composed of discussions/expressions. In the same reasoning, when section 4(2) of the SSMP forbids the 'public display' of amorous relationship between persons of similar sex, the right to freedom of expression is also attacked as provided for in section 39. Section 39 of the Nigerian Constitution provides amongst other things that:

"Every person shall be entitled to freedom of **expression**, *including freedom to hold opinions and to receive and impart ideas and information without interference."*

[Emphasis added]

The question is: "what constitutes 'expression'?". An expression consists of demonstrations and acts as well, and not necessarily spoken words[100]. Thus, a public display of affection strictly is a form of expression which is guarded by the provisions of section 39 of the Nigerian Constitution. The same position obtains in the Article 19 of the UDHR and ICCPR.

---

[99] Section 39 provides for right to freedom of expression
[100] See *Inspector-General of Police vs. All Nigeria Peoples Party and Others* (2007) AHRLR 179

Like other rights mentioned earlier. We must ask if the right to freedom of expression is absolute. The answer is in the negative, the State holds a duty to restrict expressions it considers against some societal standards, in this case – *public morality* in section 45 of the Constitution. This similar view is inherent in Article 10 of the African Charter as well, Article 10 provides that:

"Every individual shall have the right to express and disseminate his opinions **within the law.***"*
[Emphasis added]

The SSMP is a law, and both the Nigerian Constitution and the African Charter provides a basis for its existence and validity.

    ii.   *Summary of the results from the above assessment*

It must be pointed out that the provisions of the earlier discussed Criminal Code Act, Penal Code, and Shari'a law as they co-exist in Nigeria adopts the same arguments as regards the assessment above where they can so adopt. This is logical since those provisions on the proscribed sexual acts between persons of similar sex, and the surrounding acts have their validity argument (or otherwise) in the various human right provisions discussed above.

In conclusion of the "assessment" part of this work above, five rights[101] seemed to have been attacked by the

---

[101] Right to freedom from discrimination, right to privacy and family life, right to freedom of religion, right to freedom of association, right to freedom of expression

promulgation of the SSMP are highlighted, and the relevant provisions of the SSMP are also highlighted against the rights. The summary of the finding of the assessment is that the SSMP by itself is legal, but for one right which it still offends – the right to freedom from discrimination as provided under the African Charter and not the Nigerian 1999 Constitution. Clearly, rights as to privacy and family life, to freedom of religion, association, and expression are within the province of the Nigerian government to regulate. In fact, section 45 of the Nigerian 1999 Constitution providing for these rights in the first instance takes them away in certain instances, in this present case – for the purpose of regulating "public morality"[102]. The LGBTQI movement must always remember this in a possible ensuing argument that might erupt from them before a Nigerian court.

If the Nigerian government is ever questioned as regards the SSMP's validity and existence amongst several human rights often used as basis to attack the SSMP, the arguments in section 45 of the Nigerian Constitution provides a 'safe haven'. Whereas, the UDHR and ICCPR – to which Nigeria is a party – might contain a notion of *absolute* right in respect of the other rights highlighted earlier, still, the fact that the

---

[102] Section 45 provides that: 45. (1) Nothing in sections 37 (Right to privacy and family life), 38 Right to freedom of thought, conscience, and religion) , 39 (Right to freedom of expression and the press), 40 (Right to peaceful assembly and the press) and 41 of this Constitution shall invalidate any law that is reasonably justifiable in a democratic society
(a) in the interest of defense, public safety, public order, **public morality** or public health; or

Nigerian Constitution and the African Charter more closely provides a basis for the State via her laws to regulate these rights cannot be waived to the side with a backhand. At most, these provisions provide the *basis* for the validity and existence of the SSMP. The basis, forming the 'legality and validity' of the laws attacking same-sex union is, therefore (partially) established within the law. The question of whether the SSMP is a good way to exercise the duty to regulate "public morals" is another question entirely – which this work need not explore.

The truth is, the Nigerian government can always rely on the basis discussed herein and use same in arguments for the validity of the SSMP Act and other provisions of the Criminal Code Act, Penal Code Act, and the Shari'a laws of Northern States. Again, the question of whether the SSMP attacks fundamental human right as clearly seen above is in the negative although partly. The LGBTQI community in Nigeria cannot therefore totally criticize the Nigerian government for the SSMP Act and its cohorts. Also, agitations to suppress the existence of the SSMP via court actions would not resolve the issue because of these proper clarifications that find their validity within the law itself, the Constitution for that matter. The suit cited earlier contesting the SSMP Act that was dismissed by the Federal High Court in Abuja FCT would have most likely reflected the reasoning exemplified in the assessment discussed above[103].

---

[103] http://allafrica.com/stories/201410230503.html

However, from the 'assessment', it must be cited that the SSMP Act stands only on one leg considering the fact the Act still offends just one right – which is not subject to any sort of condition or regulation by the Nigerian government. The right to freedom from discrimination, especially based on 'sex' or 'gender', is an *absolute* right[104] both within the African Charter, ICCPR, and the ICESR. The provisions of section 42 of the Nigerian 1999 Constitution although contains an undertone of prevention of discrimination based on certain standards ('sex' inclusive), however, as seen above, it is not a proper basis for attacking the SSMP Act and its cohorts in the Nigerian context.

The LGBTQI community thus has to even rely on international law for the only basis of their position in Nigeria, but the African Charter should not be seen as international law in Nigeria as it has been domesticated in Nigeria and has been legislatively and judicially validated as applicable in Nigeria. This must not be considered a 'set-back' or a 'discouragement' to the LGBTQI movement, the community must be aware that the possibility of them changing the course of things on these issues in Nigeria would take a whole lot of dedication, and the effort is almost impossible but possible. This is because of the ordinary cultural, and the religious idiosyncrasies of the Nigerian people. The breakthrough of the LGBTQI even in America

---

[104] Section 42 of the Nigerian 1999 Constitution is not listed as one of those sections that could be regulated by the State in section 45. Also, other relevant international statutes do not contain provisions for such restriction or regulation.

was delayed but finally came as recent as in 2015 via the Supreme Court ruling.

As seen in America (especially in Obergefell vs. Hodges[105]), Europe, and other countries allowing the LGBTQI movement, the law is the **only** instrument the LGBTQI community could employ or stand on if they must win this *battle*. LGBTQI movement in Nigeria cannot rely on religion, morality or even nature (which supports gay tendencies) in a bid to force the Nigerian populace or the government to dance to their 'strange' tunes in the Nigerian setting. As mentioned earlier, aside from the fact that the African Charter has been domesticated and initiated into the Nigerian legal system, the Supreme Court of Nigeria[106] has ruled that *"...the African Charter is now part of the laws of Nigeria and like all other laws the Courts must uphold it."* This author wants to see a suit based on this provision in a subsequent challenge of the SSMP or its other supportive laws in a Nigerian court, not arguments built upon the Nigerian 1999 Constitution – as such arguments are destined to fail.

Succinctly, a successive challenge to the SSMP Act and its cohorts – this time by a person belonging to the LGBTQI community (so as to avoid the case been thrown out on the basis of *locus standi* again) – would be proper, if it challenges the Act based on the "right to freedom from discrimination based on *sex* and *gender*" as discussed under the African Charter. The Nigerian government must be aware that the

---

[105] *Obergefell v. Hodges*, 135 S. Ct. 2071 - 2015
[106] In *General Sani Abacha vs. Chief Gani Fawehinmi S.C. 45/1997*

SSMP Act might have scaled every other fundamental right but must resolve its position as regards the right to freedom from discrimination as promised under the African Charter. Both SSMP Act and its supportive laws and the African Charter prohibition of discrimination cannot co-exist in Nigeria, it creates a legal conundrum, and it is embarrassing. What could be done is well discussed in the "recommendation" section of this work.

There are two important issues considered to be exigent in the SSMP Act that should be highlighted here, they are one, the provisions of section 1(2). That section provides that:

"A marriage contract or civil union entered into between persons of same sex by virtue of a certificate issued by a foreign country is void in Nigeria, and any benefit accruing therefrom by virtue of the certificate shall not be enforced by any court of law."

A proper interpretation of this section would show that it has wider consequences. On the one hand, the Nigerian government is invalidating a marriage certificate issued to a same-sex couple abroad when the certificate is presented in Nigeria. In the eyes of the law, in such foreign countries, the certificate evidences 'marriage', the issue of sex or gender of parties in such marriage is oblivious to the law in such foreign country. If Nigeria has thus made such 'marriage certificate' (which is the way relevant foreign countries sees it) void, this *might* result in such foreign countries refusal to acknowledge marriage certificates issued by the Nigerian government to her citizen as well. This is the idea of 'reciprocity' between nations. We use the word 'might' because so far, there has been no such development, but clearly, as the situation lingers, the chances of this happening cannot be skirt.

If the Nigerian government strictly refuses to recognize or grant the benefits to persons who are in a civil union – by the laws of a foreign country as the US or the UK, it would mean US, UK or such foreign country would not be wrong if it refuses to recognize a marriage or marriage certificate issued by the Nigerian government as well. The fact that the Nigerian issued marriage certificate is between persons of different sex or gender would be immaterial, as the foreign country would just be reciprocating the treatment of its issued certificates as do the Nigerian government.

The relevance of section 2(1) of the SSMP Act is questioned since it affects both foreigners and Nigerians who solemnizes a same-sex marriage abroad and return to Nigeria. Whereas presently, the law must be accepted as it is, this work merely calls on the Nigerian government to examine the ramifications, especially as regards the 'possible' treatment of Nigerian citizens carrying a Nigerian marriage certificate in a foreign country. This discussion is prophetic and imminent, and the victims of the backlash of the provision would be Nigerians, not the government. The government has a duty to protect her citizen's interest both at home and abroad, and invalidating other countries marriage certificate could have adverse effects on marriage certificates carried by Nigerians abroad as well, especially in making divorce or claiming benefits or immigration to foreign countries difficult.

Another important discussion is on "support" of the LGBTQI movement, which is incriminated by section 5(3) of the SSMP Act. That section provides that:

"A person or group of persons who administers, witnesses: abets or aids the solemnization of a same-sex marriage or civil union, or **supports** *the registration, operation and sustenance of gay clubs, societies, organizations, processions or meetings in Nigeria commits an offence and is liable on conviction to a term of 10 years imprisonment."*
[Emphasis added]

While the 'support' incriminated referred to might be attached to the "association" of gays, it would seem that this provision might be interpreted widely to render actions of persons supporting the LGBTQI cause 'criminal' as well. Whereas it could be argued that supporting the LGBTQI movement alone is not incriminated, that it is the support for the association that is incriminated. The apprehension is that it is almost impossible to agitate for the LGBTQI movement without supporting their association.

Thus, where a person agitates for the allowance or accommodation of the LGBTQI cause, and in the course, the freedom of association of gay clubs, section 5(3) is saying the person is liable on conviction to a term of 10 years imprisonment. The first question is how do the Nigerian government intend to drag the international organizations as the UN and other international human right organization cited earlier, to court? Again, does this provision means that the lawyer handling *Joseph Teriah Ebah's* case thrown out by the Federal High Court is/would have been liable under this section? especially since the plaintiff, in that case, challenges the SSMP's effect on gay freedom of association. It would seem that the position of lawyers who often doubles as human right activist both in and outside the court is being incriminated by virtue of section 5(3) provisions. If section 5(3) must continue to exist, it needs some amendments to make its application reasonable, so that that provision would not incriminate the legal profession, at least.

CHAPTER 4

"Laws in Nigeria borders on 'sexual orientation', the failure of the legislature to address the position of 'gender identity' must thus be resolved in the favour of transgender persons."

-gbenga Odugbemi

*O*ther issues and Conclusions

i. *Other issues*

Aside the two issues discussed at the end of the last chapter, there are some other issues related to the LGBTQI issue that needs to be examined, especially in the Nigerian context. One of such issue is whether it is still safe to "identify" as belonging to any of those represented under the LGBTQI umbrella. Is it legal to "identify" as gay or lesbian or queer in Nigeria? this question must be answered in the affirmative. This is because the SSMP Act, and even the preceding and existing laws on homosexuality/lesbianism, do not by themselves incriminate being a gay or lesbian or queer or even transgendered. The previous and existing laws as the Penal Code Act and Criminal Code Act merely incriminate the "acts" of intercourse and "acts" surrounding it at most, the status of being gay or declaring oneself as such is still not illegal. This is so, since the SSMP Act itself incriminates mainly marriage and such other related acts, and not the "status" of being a homosexual or lesbian etc.

The Nigerian community must be made aware by the government at least that the presence of the Criminal law or Penal Code or Shari'a law or even the SSMP Act does not *ipso facto* means a person who is gay or categorized under the LGBTQI and having that status must be lynched on the street or killed as often seen on Nigerian streets. 'Status', and 'acts' – although reasonable/deducible from such 'status' – must be differentiated. Enlightening the people on this issue is the least the Nigerian government could do in this situation where a sexual minority group exercise of right has been incriminated.

The attitude of the Nigerian Police and law enforcement, whereby persons considered gay or reported as one or who declare himself as gay being maltreated automatically must also be checked. This is because it's still licit to declare one self's gender identity or sexual orientation. Without the 'acts' which are incriminated, there shouldn't be maltreatment by the police or the Nigerian masses. The government should take steps at bringing those involved in vigilante lynching of persons under the LGBTQI umbrella to justice. This is necessary, because at the end, regardless of the situation, the government still has the duty to protect her citizens. The Nigerian government must remember the causes of the Nigerian Civil War in the 1960's, germane amongst the causes is the refusal/inefficiencies of the Nigerian government to protect and secure a sect of Nigerian people.

Thus, if there are laws incriminating certain acts, those laws must **not** be interpreted to mean they also incriminate 'status' or 'self-identification'. Even if they do, the prevalence of *jungle justice* often carried out in respect of the LGBTQI community must stop. What we have are criminal laws, and the constitution still necessitates a fair trial to suspects suspected of committing a crime. The attacked sexual minority are not yet criminals, and therefore do not deserve the ailing treatments which they currently face/receive in Nigeria. The ability to be able to come out as a homosexual or lesbian or belonging to the LGBTQI community should not be considered only legal, it is also important for Nigerian legal development.

In the *Ebah's* case cited earlier, the case was thrown out because the plaintiff does not belong to the LGBTQI community. It, therefore, follows that the court requires a person who so belongs to bring the case before it. An atmosphere where such person belonging to that community can so come out must be created if we must see the court's interpretation of the laws on these issues, especially on the issue of discrimination as in the African Charter. An instance where people belonging to the LGBTQI community cannot even come out to declare themselves as so belonging has the effect of automatically closing the opportunity of a person having such status quo to bring the case before a Nigerian court. The atmosphere to so declare oneself as gay and being able to instigate a suit on the SSMP or other relevant laws validity in a Nigerian court must be allowed/created.

Also, considering the LGBTQI umbrella term, it would seem that the combined operation of the Criminal Code Act, Penal Code Act, Shari'a law, and the SSMP only incriminate surrounding acts – marriage and sexual relations by **only** lesbians, gays, queers, and bisexual persons to say the most[107]. The closest provision to being a transgender is the outward dressing by a male as female in the Penal Code applicable in the North discussed above. Thus, the position of transgender persons, queers or intersex are still left at large and unresolved.

Presently, it would seem that being a transgender, engaging in marriage based on the new sex, and engaging in intercourse and surrounding acts base on the new sex, are all licit. This, in fact, is the difference pointed out earlier between 'sexual orientation' and 'gender identity'. Laws in Nigeria borders on 'sexual orientation', the failure of the legislature to address the position of 'gender identity' must thus be resolved in the favour of transgender persons. This is so since section 36(12) requires that a law makes an act a crime before it becomes a crime, in the absence of which such act(s) would be considered licit. Even if we say the laws on sexual orientation somewhat border on gender identity as well, the delineating line is unclear and imprecise, and thus the provisions would be construed against the Nigerian government. This is the doctrine of *contra proferentem*.

Thus, in a more clear fashion, the Nigerian government must tell us the position of those people under the LGBTQI umbrella. The attitude of the society to these people whereby 'sexual orientation' – which the laws tend to frown at – must be differentiated from 'gender identity' as in transgender persons or persons having two sex organs.

---

[107] Thus, from LGBTQI, only the 'LGBQ' position and surrounding acts are being incriminated, the laws are silent on 'TI'

Considering the fact that persons having two sex organs or differing external genitalia not corresponding with the internal reproductive system — intersex — are rare, transgendered person's and willingness of persons wanting to change their sexual organs are not rare.

The question thus is: 'what is the position of transgender persons in Nigeria?' The legislature must have been *swept away* by the idea that Nigeria lacks the sophistication required for changing someone's sexual organ or carrying out gender re-assignment. However, clearly, the case of *Dapo Adaralegbe* — a male — who underwent a transgender surgery to become a female (although carried out abroad) must be resolved by the Nigerian legislature. The young Nigerian, now living in the Netherlands, and exiled by the Nigerian society and by an imprecise law must be allowed to return to Nigeria without fear of discrimination or 'attack' since there is no law on this issue. If this is the intention of the Nigerian government, it must be made clear via its legislature, if the reverse is the case, then same must be made clear, so as to normalize the misconception and the blur of the dividing line between 'sexual orientation' and 'gender identity' common amongst the Nigerian people.

A rare case where a transgender person might be considered to have fouled the law under the existing laws is in a marriage situation. If A — a man, marries B — a woman, and A later remove his genitalia and becomes a woman (— with the knowledge of B), and then return to B, the union of A and B would then amount to same–sex relationship, and therefore would be considered a crime under the SSMP Act, or the Criminal Code Act or Penal Code Act. As mentioned earlier, this is almost unusual, but it is not impossible. What we need clarification on is where A – a woman, underwent the transgender reassignment procedures, and becomes a man, and then marries B – a woman, will their marriage be considered licit or otherwise?

ii. Conclusion

This work commenced by shedding light on criminal law operation in Nigeria, and on the issue of 'sexual orientation' and 'gender identity' as conceptualized under the LGBTQI umbrella, especially as it relates to Nigeria. It confirms that the position of 'sexual orientation' is recent in interpretation but old in existence in Nigeria. The position of 'gender identity' is still unclear, but presently must be seen as a 'lacuna', and maybe should be seen as a 'hope' for the LGBTQI community. The previous laws – Criminal Code Act, the Penal Code Act, and the Shari'a law incriminates some acts surrounding 'sexual orientation' which the legislature considers contrary to 'public policy', at least to Nigerian people's belief. The new SSMP Act fosters this belief and position and makes it clear that even marriages between persons of similar sex are also criminal. It went further and makes support, association of gay clubs also criminal amongst other things.

A proper examination of the relevant laws on the issues in Nigeria, with clear explanations of the intendment of each is presented, while pointing out the areas that need amendment, especially in the "sexism" within the law. It's upon the explanations that the SSMP Act is examined against the various fundamental rights often used as the basis for challenge of the Nigerian government's assertions in a bid to see "whether the SSMP and its cohorts can co-exist with the fundamental rights provisions in Nigeria or otherwise". The relevant human rights provisions are taken from the current Nigerian 1999 Constitution as amended, and other international legislations as the ICCPR, the UDHR, the ICESCR and the African Charter.

This work places the laws on this subject, especially the SSMP on an 'assessment drill'. The assessment shows that both the government and the LGBTQI community are correct, the latter is right for challenging the Nigerian government on laws discriminating and preventing them from expressing sexual relations and even getting married. On the other hand, the Nigerian government is correct or "acting within the province of the law" when it promulgates the SSMP. In fact, the various rights often considered or referred to as been violated by the SSMP and its cohorts are within the Nigerian government to regulate. The *regulatory power* is also provided for in the Constitution and within some of the African Charter provisions especially. While it might be said that it is a sad day for the LGBTQI community, in Nigeria at least. The only iota of hope for that community lies in the clear discriminatory tendencies of the SSMP and its cohorts, since freedom from discrimination is guaranteed by the African Charter, and that section is free from 'regulation' by the Nigerian government. The SSMP can be argued to have incited discrimination.

Clearly, as described above, the SSMP and its cohorts offend the African Charter, and all other international legislation suggesting non-discrimination based on sex or gender to which Nigeria is a party. A viable challenge of the SSMP Act and its cohorts' argument must, therefore, be channeled towards the "discriminatory line of reasoning" – if a positive result is expected by the LGBTQI community. In essence, non-governmental organizations as *Initiative for Equal Rights* by *Bisi Alimi*, international organizations, and relevant countries from the West must accept the SSMP and its cohorts as promulgated by the Nigerian government as an exercise of her *legal power* ensured by law in Nigeria. The Nigerian government, on the other hand, must also note that a possible way to challenge the SSMP and its cohorts is questioning them for being discriminatory base on sex and/or gender. This is true since the Nigerian government shot herself in the leg when it domesticated the *overwhelming* African Charter.

Later, this work also shows that the position of transgendered persons or collectively – the 'gender orientation' position is not provided for in Nigeria. Thus, whereas the Nigeria community might frown at an adventure engaged in changing one's sexual organ etc, transgendered person (MTF[108] or FTM[109]) can engage in the proscribed

---

[108] Male to Female
[109] Female to Male

acts by the SSMP Act and its cohorts acting under the guise of the new sex – this is correct, at least as at when this work is written. This is an interpretation which the Nigerian government must either correct or condone until such correction.

CHAPTER 5

The legislature must evolve with time, grapple with current trends, the legal developments in the world, and exhibit same in law-making.
   -gbenga Odugbemi

Recommendations, and Arising Issues

Whereas it is doubtful whether the Nigerian government would be willing to implement the recommendations that would be discussed here; still, a work as this would be incomplete or counter-productive without a recommendation section.

The idea of sexism within Nigerian laws must be removed. Certain provisions of the Criminal Code Act, Penal Code Act and State's Shari'a law provisions (as discussed above) makes some of the crimes discussed committable by male persons alone, even when they are now capable of being committed by females. The masculine gender must not be seen always as the only possible perpetrator of crimes on these issues and even in respect of other crimes. The legislature must evolve with time, grapple with current trends, the legal developments in the world, and exhibit same in law-making. This recommendation extends to section 357 of the Criminal Code Act which still makes only a male person capable of committing rape.

In the same line, 'consent' as used in some provisions of the laws as section 285 of the Penal Code Act and 130 of the Shari'a law as in Zamfara State cited earlier, must be removed as same do not properly reflect the idea/vision deposited in the later SSMP Act. The legislature is confusing us, is it that when there is *consent*, there's no crime or consent regardless equates crime? From the idea of the recent SSMP, consent between parties do not by itself decriminalize the acts the law makes criminal, but the discrepancies within the law on the subject must be made clear.

It is doubtful whether Shari'a law could be amended, but a sentence of 'stoning' for being gay and exhibiting the acts while married is rather excessive. It puts Nigeria some steps backward in the legal scene. We are no more in the primitive age. Thus, if Shari'a law had been agreed amongst academics and scholars as being customary law, it might be said that same would be subjected to the "repugnancy tests", and a death penalty by stoning will not survive such test. The Nigerian government must emulate the situation in Article 8 of the US Constitution – forbidding "cruel and unusual punishment". Stoning a spouse to death for being gay and exhibiting the attitude during the subsistence of a valid Islamic marriage is barbaric, cruel and unusual. It is not different from a punishment as public disembowelment or dismemberment. The government can control Islamic law applicability and make some reservations where necessary especially so as same can be in tune with what obtains in a civilized society.

The attitude of the Federal High Court in Abuja throwing a suit challenging the SSMP Act while revered – because it has a basis in law – must also not become a trend for other courts in Nigeria. Luckily, the case was thrown out at the High Court level, not a higher court level as the Court of Appeal. It thus means that, if a subsequent case on the subject most likely in another State High Court is brought, the latter court need not follow the Federal High Court's decision as a precedent – because both courts are on the same level. We recommend that if such case comes up before another court, futuristically, such court should try (even if there are legal technicalities that might render the case not viable) and make some pronouncements on the legality or otherwise of the SSMP and its cohorts. This is because activists and persons belonging to the LGBTQI community are waiting patiently (in private) on a legal interpretation of these laws; since these laws are just dormant for the time being, we need some judicial interpretation of the law(s).

From the latter argument on marriage certificates, the benefits that follow, and the certificate's recognition as between Nigeria and foreign countries. As discussed above, section 1(2) in the SSMP Act could result in an imminent friction between Nigeria and countries that have legalized gay marriage. It is important for the Nigerian legislature to examine its actual *'fear'* and look into the effect of that section of the law. This writer is not aware of such *'fear'* the Nigerian government might nurture, but we can point to two of such fears. More likely, the Nigerian government might have been of the opinion that if same-sex marriages are incriminated in Nigeria, Nigerian gays can boycott the law, travel abroad – where such marriage is allowed – then return and present their certificate of marriage in Nigeria, then require same to be recognized. Truly, this would render the SSMP's aim futile, useless and ineffective. Another likely fear is that the Nigerian government wants to erase all traces of same-sex relationship in Nigeria, and even guard against any possibility of its introduction via foreign marriage or marriage certificates etc.

Whereas these fears are reasonable considering the aim of the SSMP as explained in the Act's preamble. We recommend that this section should take international relations between Nigeria and other foreign countries where same-sex marriages are allowed into consideration. A more reasonable way to do is by giving recognition to the marriage certificates of couples of same-sex union from foreign countries where the couples are originally foreigners (or non-Nigerians). In other words, the provisions of section 1(2) should not apply to foreign same-sex couples. This is for the likely consequence that if their certificates are rendered void in Nigeria because the parties are of the same-sex, certificates issued in Nigeria where the couples are persons of different sex *might* also be rendered void abroad as well.

The adverse effect to Nigerian couples of different sexual orientation abroad would be more than that of foreigners in Nigeria since Nigerian same-sex couples are few anyway. However, to prevent boycotting the SSMP Act, Nigerians who travel abroad for the purpose of engaging in a same-sex marriage and have obtained a certificate to the effect should receive the treatment prescribed in section 1(2). In other words, a Nigerian cannot hold the Nigerian nationality and engage in same-sex marriage abroad, and then come to Nigeria to claim benefits for the marriage. These two recommendations might seem as laborious checks, but still, they should be incorporated into the provisions of section 1(2) so as to aver imminent friction in Nigeria's international relation with Western countries.

Secondly, on the result of the assessment of the SSMP Act in relation to fundamental rights existing in Nigeria. Since section 42 is not within the Nigerian government to regulate via section 45 or any other law for that matter. Also, since the right to freedom from discrimination based on any standard, sex or gender inclusive should not be conditional, but absolute, and because a State must ensure equality amongst its citizens regardless of their sexual orientation or gender. Also, because the African Charter supposes a non-discriminatory State free from discrimination based on sex or gender; and because Nigeria has domesticated the African Charter. The Nigerian government could do two things.

One, find a way to make section 42 looks 'regulatory' in the constitution. This perhaps is a tedious task – because of the votes required by the legislature to amend the right. Aside from this, this effort is of course not the best route for the Nigerian government. This is so because the African Charter is the main basis for a possible attack of the SSMP and its supportive laws. So, section 42 may thus be amended to reflect Article 2 of the African Charter and made regulatory via section 45 of the Constitution as well.

Another way out is leaving the African Union or finding a way to renounce the African Charter since it is the organization's Charter – the African Charter – that is making the SSMP and its supportive law invalid/illegal. If the Nigerian government must hinge on the continued operation of the SSMP Act – a clearly discriminatory law – then, it behooves the Nigerian government to find a way a make 'discrimination' based on the standards listed permissible. It is either the Nigerian government do this or repeal the SSMP Act because it is discriminatory of a minority group in Nigeria anyway, why allow a continued existence/applicability of a discriminatory law?

(A case for the LGBTQI)
A more reasonable and well-founded recommendation is for the Nigerian government to refuse to exercise its power under section 45 of the Constitution in respect of all the rights affected and refrain from using the SSMP Act as a regulatory policy/tool under that section of the Constitution. The fact that the Nigerian government has the power to regulate association, private life of citizens, their expression, or religion in a bid to maintain 'public morality' does not mean the government must exercise such power. While agreeing that *morality* is relative, the Nigerian government must be aware that the percentage of those captured under the LGBTQI community is a minority part of the Nigerian population – a population more than 170 million. We recommend that the Nigerian government as a [political] State entrusted with the duty to ensure equality amongst its

citizens should refrain from regulating who can marry who and what churches do or even religious issues *in toto*.

The LGBTQI movement has a root in the idea of *consent* anyway, so why should the government interfere with the abilities of adults to consent – as regards sexual relationship or marriage? Especially when such consent and the activities involved do not affect a third party in no way. It is like intruding into a normal contract between two parties. Although from a religious plinth or morality plinth in the Nigerian context, allowing same-sex marriages might be wrong, the Nigerian government should refrain from these two standards and use the most consistent tool which is 'law' – as employed by more developed countries as the USA.

Nigeria is not a religious or moral State, it is a legal State; morality, religion or cultural dispositions do not apply in Nigerian courts, the judges and lawyers seek to apply the law in our courts. Law suggests and proposes that people should be treated equally, the minorities and the majorities in the society should be treated alike, and given the same opportunity, opportunity to marry inclusively, and to choose their own gender or sexuality. Perhaps, this explains why the Nigerian government was able to scale all of the other human rights in our assessment above but was unable to scale the right to freedom from discrimination. We propose that the Nigerian government use "law" as a yardstick instead of using the "religion" or "morality" standard in refuting the clamor of the LGBTQI movement.

The people captured under the LGBTQI community are not asking for anything that's abnormal, they are only asking for the same treatment and not to be discriminated against – all of which has their undertone in the Nigerian constitution and international legislations Nigeria is committed to. There is perhaps, no proper basis to rebut prevention of discrimination on any basis in law. Hopefully, this recommendation is not viewed as a 'support' for the LGBTQI community as somewhat incriminated in section 5(3) of the SSMP Act. This recommendation is a recommendation, and nothing more, it's not a support or agitation whatsoever.

CHAPTER 6

"...must persons claiming to belong to the opposite sex undergo a complete gender reassignment surgery before he/she claims that sex and use public bathrooms? will allowing it not confuse the little ones growing up?..."

   -gbenga Odugbemi

The Ramifications of Legalizing the LGBT Movement in Nigeria

The writer was thrown in a sort of dilemma on the importance of this chapter – portraying the ramifications of legalizing the LGBT movement in Nigeria. On the one hand, this chapter might be misperceived as showing the 'negative' side of legalizing the movement – thereby supporting the Nigerian position – which forbids the movement. On the other hand, it might be misperceived as counter-argumentative; since this writer had in the previous chapter tend to advocate for legalizing the movement – since criminalizing it does not seem to be *in tandem* with the law. However, at the end, it must be understood that this book is a discussion, a law discussion, presenting a robust and full view on the legality of the LGBT movement or otherwise. Thus, for the discussion to be "robust and full", it behooves the writer to discuss the ramifications of legalizing the movement, especially by construing the problems countries which have legalized the movement are currently facing.

No doubt, all the countries legalizing the LGBT movement have been faced with several questions – which constitute a snag to the legality of the LGBT movement as we shall see later. It must be understood that these problems and questions should not ordinarily be construed as a reason not to advance a human right. It is better to advance a human right and find solutions to the problem it might create than suppress the right for reasons as the preventable 'negative' ramifications. The refusal to advance such right should not be the ideal way, especially if the 'negative' ramifications do not outweigh the merits of advancing the right or could be subdued with less cost/mechanisms.

On the top list of the consequence of legalizing the LGBT movement, homosexuality and being bi-sexual especially is the increment in sexually transmitted infection and diseases amongst the gay and bi-sexual people, and its spread to others. The bi-sexual people contributes to its increment amongst the general populace since they are bi-sexual. The high risk of STDs and STIs amongst the LGBT community is notorious. Without overstressing the issue, the assertions, findings, and statistics amongst the LGBT movement speaks for itself. In the US for example, the CDC[110] asserts that: "…while anyone who has sex can get an STD, sexually active gay, bisexual and other men who have sex with men (MSM) are at greater risk. In addition to having higher rates of syphilis, more than half of all new HIV infections occur among MSM."[111] Also, *Guoyu Tao* did a research titled: "Sexual Orientation and Related Viral Sexually Transmitted Disease Rates Among US Women Aged 15 to 44 Years",

---

[110] Centers for Disease Control and Prevention, a national public health Institute in the US
[111] See: http://www.cdc.gov/msmhealth/std.htm

and found out that: "Bisexual women have a higher risk of contracting HIV than women who have sex with women exclusively, because they also have sex with men whose semen contains proteins that serve as an extremely efficient carrier of the virus. Among women, viral STD rates among bisexual-identifying women aged 15 to 44 years were almost three times higher than women who have sex with women exclusively."[112]

Lastly, in an article written by *Kristena Ducre* in 2015, titled: "Out of the Closet, Into the Clinic: LGBT STD Statistics", she found and confirmed that: "Statistics show that men who have sex with men— whether they identify as gay, bisexual, or other— have a higher risk of contracting an STD than any demographic...Approximately 3.5 percent of Americans identify as gay, bisexual, or other. Despite making up a small fraction of the population, men who have sex with men (MSM) account for more than half of all new cases of HIV each year...Gay and bisexual men account for the majority of those cases of syphilis (nearly 75 percent)...Gay and bisexual men are known to have higher risks of catching an STD, but lesbian and bisexual women aren't free from risk."[113]

This is an undeniable consequence legalizing the LGBT movement would (not could) have. The problem could have been reduced if there are no bisexual persons. The presence of bi-sexual persons increases the likelihood of heterosexuals

---

[112] See: https://www.ncbi.nlm.nih.gov/pmc/articles/PMC2377304/
[113] See: https://www.stdcheck.com/blog/lgbt-std-statistics/

being susceptible to contracting the various STIs and STDs; and when a higher percentage of gay people and heterosexuals have STIs and STDs, sexual relationships would become highly unsafe[114]. Still, it must be noted that engaging in activities that expose one to infections/diseases is a choice, but just after that supposition is the function of the government to ensure public health. Thus whether incriminating the LGBT movement entirely is a preventive measure or whether other mechanisms can be put in place is another discussion entirely which we need not discuss here. The aim of this chapter is to highlight the ramifications of legalizing the LGBT movement.

The next ramification worthy of note is the confluence of legalizing the LGBT movement and religion – Islamic religion especially – in Nigeria. As argued somewhere in this book, in chapter 2, Nigeria is more of an Islamic State. Aside this, an Islamic insurgent group – Boko Haram – has been tormenting the country since 2011, hitherto. As notoriously known, the assertion of this group is that western education is a sin – a translation from the Hausa language predominant in the North Eastern part of Nigeria – where the group is most active. The LGBT idea of course (in the Nigeria setting) is a western idea, although this point could be debated. The point we are trying to make is that legalizing the LGBT would create a Pyrrhic victory for the LGBT movement themselves, as they would also be continually

---

[114] Abstinence would be the only prevention method then, since even condoms and other contraceptives are not 100 percent prevention mechanisms

exposed to dangers by the insurgent group. This assertion is a possibility. However, the case of the Orlando Gay Night Club shooting in America in June 2016 creates a notion of the possibility of an attack on the LGBT movement in Nigeria.

Succinctly, legalizing the LGBT movement in Nigeria would most likely have the effect of infuriating the Boko Haram group – which the Nigerian government do not seem to be capable of conquering without negotiation and/amnesty[115] – and this can lead to further attacks. Aside from the possibility of the Boko Haram group becoming more dangerous towards the LGBT movement, the ordinarily Nigerian society is religious and would be ready to issue lashes towards persons involved in the movement. Still, it would be better if the Boko Haram issue is being resolved first, then the legality of the LGBT movement can then face the wrath of other religious groups in Nigeria – which to some extent can still be tolerated compared to the violent attacks the Boko Haram assault is infested with.

Another ramification that is imminent in an LGBT accommodating society is as regards the prison system. This consequence relates to the transgender arm of the movement. Thus, the question beckons on what prison should a male who is a transgender be incarcerated? In the US, the issue is still undergoing serious debates, recently, the US prohibits imprisoning transgender inmates in cells based

---

[115] http://www.nytimes.com/2016/09/17/world/africa/nigeria-boko-haram-chibok.html?_r=0

on birth anatomy[116]. In this regard, the consequences of incarcerating a male transgender in a female prison could be disastrous, in fact, this is the fear raised in a US State – North Carolina – as regards the use of public bathrooms. Thus, must persons claiming to belong to the opposite sex undergo a complete gender reassignment surgery before he/she claims that sex and use public bathrooms? will allowing it not confuse the little ones growing up?, what about the fear of rape?. Just, what bathroom should a transgender person use in public? The one he/she is assigned at birth or the one he/she now claims? These issues are causing lots of controversies, and the west seems to wish there is a straight-jacket solution to the problems as they continue to battle with the issues.

Just beside all these issues is the Olympics games. The questions are: in what game should a transgender person participate? will he/she participate in a game designed for males even when she had been through gender reassignment into a male, and vice versa? Sometimes in January 2016 before the just concluded Olympics in Brazil, it is announced that "Transgender athletes to be allowed to compete as the other sex in the Olympics without having reassignment surgery"[117]. In any way, the consequence of this is that: prior male now saying they are female would

---

[116] https://www.theguardian.com/us-news/2016/mar/24/transgender-prison-gender-identity-anatomy-doj-rules
[117] http://www.dailymail.co.uk/news/article-3412969/Olympics-change-policies-allow-transgender-athletes-compete-without-having-gender-reassignment-surgery.html

compete with their 'female counterparts' without the gender reassignment surgery.

Unfortunately, it seems the Olympics committee, the NCAA in the US and such other bodies adopting this idea seems to not appreciate the issue involved. The issue is not the athletes undergoing gender reassignment surgery, the issue is whether it is fair to allow a biological male person now saying she is female compete with other biological females. In this writer's view, a separate or an additional set of games for transgender persons would solve this problem, rather than subjecting biological females for example to a competition with biological males. It is kind of fallacious and hypocritical for the LGBT movement to request and clamor for justice, and then subject others to injustice or unfairness.

Conclusively, as mentioned above, the fact that these ramifications are inherent or imminent as can be seen in places where the LGBT movement has been legalized should not automatically mean the Nigerian government must not revisit the law incriminating the LGBT movement. The problems are such that solutions could be improvised in solving them. Western countries are grappling and trying to solve most of the problems, and perhaps the Nigerian government can wait till these issues are settled/resolved before venturing into legalizing the movement – considering the fact that Nigeria is a developing State. This writer and most LGBT movement advocates (in Nigeria) would agree with a promised legalization of the LGBT movement in the future, but not that it is legal to incriminate the movement in law.

As mentioned above, most of the problems can be catered for, the Olympics issue can be easily resolved if a separate or additional set of games is created for transgender persons. The same solution would go for a prison system for transgender persons. Although a creation a new prison system in Nigeria is an idea full of many impediments, as even the current and available prisons are themselves trying to perform the functions they were created for. The spread of STIs and STDs amongst the persons involved in the movement can be prevented by providing adequate sexual education, encouraging STI and STD test too often to prevent further spread, providing good health care system etc. The use of public bathrooms adopts the proposed solution mentioned earlier, and it can also be resolved easily if a separate public bathroom is created for transgender persons. The government must accept these responsibilities as the wages of validating a human right – which would be revered and understandable.

References

- A.I. ABIKAN, *"The Application of Islamic Law in Civil Causes in Nigerian Courts"*, Journal of International and Comparative Law, (June 2002) 6 JICL. Pages 88-115
- ALI MAZRUI, *"The Trial of Christopher Okigbo"*, African Writers Series (London: Heinemann 1971)
- ANTHONY F. LANG Jr., *"Punishment, Justice and International Relations: Ethics and Order After the Cold War"*, [Published by: Routledge, Oct 16, 2009]
- CHINUA ACHEBE, *"There Was A Country (A Personal History of Biafra)"*, Penguin Books, 2012
- JOSH SAGER, *"Refuting Anti-Gay Rights Argument"* available at: **https://theprogressivecynic.com/debunking-right-wing-talking-points/refuting-anti-gay-rights-arguments/**
- JADESOLA LOKULO-SODIPE, Oluwatoyin Akintola, Clement Adebamowo, *"Introduction to the legal system of Nigeria"*, 2014. Available at: **http://elearning.trree.org/mod/page/view.php?id=142**
- L. A. KELANI, *"Islamic Law and the Customary/Native Law: A Line of Distinction"*, Unilorin Shariah Journal, Vol. 1, Dec 2000
- WRIGHT, VALERIE (November 2010). "Evo\nty vs. Severity of Punishment". The Sentencing Project. Retrieved 13 October 2012
- Y. K SAADU, *"Islamic Law is NOT Customary Law"*, 1997 Kwara Law Review, Vol. 6.
- "The Holy Qur'an enjoins the sanctity and fortitude of conjugal ties." See: **http://umma.ws/Fatwa/marriage/**
- **http://www.thereligionofpeace.com/pages/quran/adultery-stoning.aspx**
- **http://thestreetjournal.org/2012/02/nigerian-professors-homosexual-son-becomes-woman-in-spain/**
- **http://www.vanguardngr.com/2016/03/photos-buhari-hosts-international-islamic-conference-in-abuja/**
- **www.f-law.net/law/showthread.php/37487-Shari-ah-Penal-Code-Law-Zamfara-State-Of-Nigeria-January-2000**
- "Nigeria Gay Trial Disrupted by Thousands of Protesters", Jan. 22, 2014, available at www.huffingtonpost.com/2014/01/22/nigeria-gay-trial-protest_n_4645942.html

- http://www.inquisitr.com/1749672/florida-churches-are-doing-what-many-county-clerks-refuse-to-do-solemnize-gay-marriages/
- https://www.hrw.org/news/2014/01/14/nigeria-anti-lgbt-law-threatens-basic-rights
- http://www.hrc.org/blog/nigeria-outlaws-same-sex-marriage-and-lgbt-organizing
- http://www.tedxliberdade.com/topic/
- http://yubanet.com/world/Nigeria_Anti-Gay_Bill_Threatens_Democratic_Reforms_52100.php#.Vv1lTaQrLIU
- http://news.yahoo.com/law-nigeria-bans-same-sex-marriage-220259835.html
- http://76crimes.com/2013/06/03/nigeria-ban-on-lawyers-for-gays-all-same-sex-roommates/
- http://www.theparadigmng.com/2014/01/18/nigerian-gay-pastor-rev-rowland-on-the-run-relocate-to-the-uk/
- http://www.aidspan.org/gfo_article/global-fund-and-unaids-urge-nigeria-reconsider-new-anti-gay-law
- http://www.ohchr.org/EN/Issues/SRHRDefenders/Pages/Declaration.aspx
- http://www.nigeriarights.gov.ng/UniversalDeclaration.php
- https://www.escr-net.org/resources/section-5-background-information-icescr
- http://www.buzzfeed.com/lesterfeder/nigerian-court-throws-out-challenge-to-anti-lgbt-law#.qs1B4xRao
- http://www.medicalnewstoday.com/articles/232363.php
- http://www.slate.com/blogs/outward/2014/02/24/gambian_president_calls_gays_ungodly_vermin_how_america_should_respond.html
- http://www.livescience.com/17913-advantages-gay-parents.html
- http://www.bbc.com/news/uk-politics-37257005
- https://www.washingtonpost.com/news/acts-of-faith/wp/2015/07/01/why-the-episcopal-church-is-still-debating-gay-marriage/
- http://www.inquisitr.com/1749672/florida-churches-are-doing-what-many-county-clerks-refuse-to-do-solemnize-gay-marriages/
- http://allafrica.com/stories/201410230503.html
- http://www.cdc.gov/msmhealth/std.htm

- https://www.ncbi.nlm.nih.gov/pmc/articles/PMC2377304/
- https://www.stdcheck.com/blog/lgbt-std-statistics/
- http://www.nytimes.com/2016/09/17/world/africa/nigeria-boko-haram-chibok.html?_r=0
- https://www.theguardian.com/us-news/2016/mar/24/transgender-prison-gender-identity-anatomy-doj-rules
- http://www.dailymail.co.uk/news/article-3412969/Olympics-change-policies-allow-transgender-athletes-compete-without-having-gender-reassignment-surgery.html

About the Author

Gbenga Odugbemi is a lawyer and a legal writer. He garnered his legal education at Babcock University, the Nigerian Law School – both in Nigeria, and the University of Edinburgh, UK. He has interest in all aspects of law.

www.ingramcontent.com/pod-product-compliance
Lightning Source LLC
Chambersburg PA
CBHW021433170526
45164CB00001B/229